Understanding Anti Money Laundering

A Concise Guide for Financial Personnel and Business Managers

Brittney Mann

Table of Contents

Introduction

Many readers of this book may be involved with a financial institution as part of an anti–money laundering (AML) program or government agency investigating money laundering. As far as financial institution AML programs, I have found that many of these programs do a great job covering the basics; however, sometimes they lack in the area of truly explaining why the employee does the specific job assigned. Sure, AML employees have learned to click this box and select that radio button—a sort of "if this, then that" programing for AML personnel. I have often enjoyed seeing that "light bulb" moment when I have explained to AML employees the reasons why they click this button and select that box. It helps to know a little about the nomenclature of money laundering, what happened before a financial institution became involved, and how it came to be that they have this incident report or alert currently sitting in front of them. You should have at least a rudimentary understand what the bad guys did, how they did it, and why they did it that way. You should be clear on how that particular activity gave rise to an alert coming across the desk of an AML employee in some small credit union in Smallville, USA, or a big-boy bank in Manhattan. Further, understanding what happens after a financial institution completes its mission and information is handed off will make your notation of that information substantially more thorough and complete.

The other side of that coin stands law enforcement agencies and personnel who understand wire taps, subpoenas, and pick-ups yet may have little experience in how a financial institution operates. Knowing the ins and outs of the Bank Secrecy Act and how AML programs are applied could be a huge asset to law enforcement. It is a major asset for law enforcement to be familiar with the methods of filtering, documentation, and record keeping at a financial institution.

That leads into another important factor: the dynamics between the three major players on Team Good Guy. The players are the financial institutions, the regulators, and law enforcement. They each have various responsibilities and perspectives. At times, they have been at odds with each other. However, from my perspective, the dynamics have gotten much better over the last few years with the introduction of the FFIEC manual, FinCEN's new reporting forms, and more communication across the board between the financial institutions, regulators, and law enforcement. If 9/11 is the day that changed everything, then we have come a long way in a relatively short period of time to bring all these various money-laundering fighters together and zero in on the best way to fight the battle.

With this book I hope to deliver to you some insight into various money-laundering methods and an awareness of the AML process. You are now part of a law enforcement money-laundering ride-a-long. I include real stories where I can and offer my opinion based on my education and experience.

---

1. What Is Money Laundering?

The Basics You Need to Know

✉

(1)

The term *money laundering* was coined in the famous 1920s gangster era of American history. Between gambling, prostitution, and sales of prohibition alcohol, there was a lot of cash that required laundering. In other words, a method or methods had to be developed so that the government did not become suspicious about the true nature of a gangster's funds. The major headache that gangsters faced was that the money they "earned" was in the form of cash currency—and often in small-denomination bills or coins. If the funds were put into the bank, then questions would be asked by the bank and ultimately the government. Further, storing large amounts of money in low-value coins is a physical and logistic nightmare. So, the gangsters created businesses, one of which involved slot machines and another of which was laundromats. The coins could be used to "gamble" and to "wash clothes" Of course, the number of coins actually used far exceeded the true amount gambled or used at the laundromat, and it was made to appear that more gambling or more clothes were washed than actually were. And so, it is said, the term *money laundry* was born.

While the term *money laundering* has been around since the early 20th century, the ideas and economics of money laundering have been around for thousands of years. Four thousand years ago, in China and other Asian countries, ruling parties took advantage of merchants to get more funds. In turn, the merchants became skilled at moving money around without it being identified and seized.

Turning "Bad" Money into "Legitimate" Money

Money laundering is the practice of integrating the proceeds of crime into the legitimate mainstream of the financial community by concealing its origin. (Various countries may have additional stipulations in order to prosecute lawbreakers.) In other, more simplistic terms, money laundering is making dirty money appear to be legitimate. That's why it's called laundering, as in cleaning. Money laundering may appear to many people like a sophisticated international game of intrigue and mystery—a chess match between good and bad and to the victor goes the spoils. But make no mistake about it; there are some evil people behind the act of money laundering. Quite often there is a fatal outcome to those engaged in or surrounded by money laundering (think drug cartels and terrorist organizations that have a lot of money to launder).

> **Definition**
> Money laundering is the practice of integrating the proceeds of criminal enterprises into the legitimate mainstream of the financial community.

So, it's all about making bad money appear legitimate. That is a simple and wonderful definition; however, I can hear you now: "So what?" "Big deal!" "Why should I care?" And, the always intuitive, "WTF?" I plan to respond to all those questions, but let's start with a basic question: Why does a bad guy have to launder his money in the first place?

Bad guys need to launder for several reasons.

- The legitimate financial system is perhaps the safest place for the bad guy to keep his fortune. Believe it or not, if Bad Guy A kept his loot under that mattress, then guaranteed, Bad Guy B would rip him off. Honor among thieves? No such thing.

- The bad guy needs to move the money around the globe quickly. That is exactly what banks and money service businesses are set up to do (legitimately).

- The bad guy, with his newfound fortune that is a result of whatever dastardly deeds he has committed, finds himself in a position where he can't go spending his money haphazardly. Doing so would bring suspicion upon him by neighbors, businesses, gatekeepers, financial institutions, and government agents. Those people would say, "How did this guy make so much money that affords him his lifestyle?" Once the government begins to dig under the rocks, they would find no means of income for Mr. Bad Guy. Then they would seriously examine his credentials and his ability to have made all that money.

For all of you anti-money laundering (AML) purists out there, I can add one more element to the definition of money laundering that is usually left out. The Palermo Convention defines money laundering as follows:

"The conversion or transfer of property, knowing it is derived from a criminal offense, for the purpose of concealing or disguising its illicit origin or of assisting any person who is involved in the commission of the crime to evade the legal consequences of his actions."[1]

> **Note**
> The Palermo Convention is a resolution adopted by the United Nations Convention against Transnational Organized Crime that was held in Palermo, Italy, in 2000.

Note the key word in that quote: *knowing*. In other words, some players, such as smurfs,[2] mules, reshippers,[3] or some other low-level wanna-be bad guys, may not actually be considered money launderers. For example, someone might be given the job to pick up a gray Chevy in parking area G, spot 177, at Terminal 5 at JFK Airport in New York. He is told to drive the car to the Paramus Park Mall in New Jersey, park in the back of lot 7, and wait for a blue Dodge minivan. When the minivan arrives, they park next to each other, and a couple of suitcases are switched from one car to another. The driver of the minivan has orders to drive to another location and follow further instructions. So, what is going on here? It could be a lot of different things with various endings. However, the main concept here is that none of these drivers "knows" what is going on or what their load is. They are just collecting a few dollars for obeying instructions and driving a car from here to there without any idea of what's in the vehicle or suitcase. Now, if the load is illegally obtained money, did they know? Can they therefore be charged with money laundering? Depending upon the circumstances and any outstanding evidence, probably not.

Interestingly, *mules*—people whose job it is to simply transport illegal goods, whether money, guns, or drugs—have been used for thousands of years. One of the first usages of encrypted messages dates back thousands of years to the ancient Roman Empire. When a coded message needed to be sent (keeping in mind that sending a message hundreds of miles might take several weeks), the head of a messenger (a mule) would be shaved. The message would be tattooed onto his head and his hair allowed to grow back, and then he was sent on his way. If he were to be stopped by the enemy, he appeared to carry no messages. Upon his arrival at his destination, his head would be shaved, and the message would be delivered. So, this concept has been going on for a long time. That is what I call a time-tested procedure!

Professional money launderers are smart to use mules so they can limit the amount of information that any one person in their employ has. In AML, and in particular in fraud, we talk a lot about the separation of duties. Well, in any self-respecting drug-dealing operation, the money and the drugs never meet, nor do the mules have any clue what anyone else is doing. This limits the damage when law enforcement crashes their party.

Money Laundering All Around Us

Before we get any deeper into the subject of money laundering, I'd like to take a moment to provide you with a basic understanding of just how prevalent money laundering is. I'm sure you will be familiar with various types of fraud from advanced-fee scams (think of the e-mail you get from Nigeria) to work-from-home scams to Ponzi (pyramid) schemes (Bernie Madoff, among others). These are visual and easily comprehended by the masses. We all either have been victimized or know someone who has been victimized by some type of fraudulent scheme. However, money laundering is quite the opposite. By its very nature it is covert and stealthy. For this reason, most of us never see money laundering nor realize that we are all victims of the money-laundering process. The masses don't see the laundering process like they do a fraud scheme. It's easy to hate fraudsters who are ripping off the elderly with various scams. However, rarely do you hear the cry of "string 'em up" with reference to your friendly neighborhood money launderer.

> *$2 Trillion: The scope of money laundering Just how big an issue is money laundering? Well, it is estimated to be about a $2 trillion a year industry. Just to help you conceptualize how much that is, let's look at it this way. A single $1 bill (US) is approximately .0004 of an inch. One million single dollar bills would be approximately 2/3 of a mile high, or about the size of two Empire State Buildings stacked on top of each other. The height of one trillion dollar bills would be approximately 134,000 miles high. That is a little more than halfway to the moon. So, $2 trillion would take us right up*

to the Sea of Tranquility. One small step for man, huh?

As you move forward to other chapters, please remember that for an event to be considered money laundering, a predicate crime[4] must have taken place (a list of specified unlawful activities is located in the Appendix). However, the various methods of money laundering make it virtually impossible to determine whether the suspect is a money launderer, tax evader, or terrorist financier. The reason is because many of the methods used to move money around in a stealthy fashion are similar or the same. Usually, in the early stages of investigation, it is not known which one, if any, your suspect might be. More often than not, that determination will come from law enforcement in the latter stages of an AML investigation.

Note
Especially in the early stages, it's nearly impossible to tell whether an illegal transfer of money is garden-variety laundering, tax evasion, or funding for terrorists.

How Money Is Laundered

It was mentioned previously that money laundering is the process by which a large amount of illegally obtained money is given the appearance of having originated from a legitimate source. In other words, criminals construct the appearance that ill-gotten gains are actually theirs to spend. It allows the criminals to maintain control over their illegal proceeds and ultimately to provide a legitimate cover story for their source of income. In other words, it allows them to enjoy the fruits of their crimes. Money laundering usually involves a sequence of numerous transactions used as a form of smoke screen to hide the true source of financial assets so that those financial gains may be used without exposing the criminals. Money laundering plays a fundamental role in facilitating the ambitions of the drug trafficker, the terrorist, the organized criminal, and the insider dealer, as well as the many others who need to evade the kind of attention from the authorities that sudden wealth brings from illegal actions. By engaging in this type of activity, it is hoped to place the proceeds beyond the reach of any asset forfeiture laws.

For example, a subject claims to be a hot dog vender in Central Park, and each month he deposits $50,000 into his account at the bank. Either the subject does one heck of a lot of hot dog business or there is something fishy about his hot dogs. This would be suspicious to the bank, to bank-regulating authorities, and to law enforcement. Some official would want to know where the money actually came from, and an investigation would begin. This is not what a money launderer wants. He wants to conduct banking transactions that do not bring about suspicion.

Why would this be suspicious to the bank? The bank would perform its due diligence (enhanced due diligence) on this customer. As part of its Customer Identification Program, the bank would perform a horizontal (a transaction timeline) and vertical analysis of the account and other similar accounts (comparing activity to other hot dog vendors). Would the numbers seem right? Is $50,000 per month the average of other hot dog vendors? Has this vendor ever done that amount of business before? Could there be a legitimate reason? Sure. Perhaps this hot dog vendor has bought out nine other hot dog vendors and he is now the Hot Dog King of Central Park. However, there should be proof of that. If not, he would certainly be a person of interest.

In later chapters, I will outline the events that surround a money-laundering investigation to give you a better idea of how bankers and law enforcement officials uncover money launderers.

Tax evaders also launder money, perhaps for a bit of a different reason. A tax evader usually makes money legitimately, but she does not want the Internal Revenue Service to discover her financial gains so she can avoid paying taxes. Are tax evaders violating any money-laundering statutes? No, there needs to be a predicate offense (such as drug dealing) to initiate a money-laundering case. This is commonly referred to as a specified unlawful activity.

Why AML Efforts Are Important

Other than crimes of passion and terroristic acts, most crimes are committed for some type of financial profit. Financial crimes affect everyone. Money laundering undermines the legitimate financial sector and can weaken financial institutions. Developing countries might be vulnerable because they might not be as selective about their sources of capital and organized crime can become entrenched. Higher taxes for the rest of us result when criminals do not pay taxes on their activities. Money laundering also creates higher operational costs to businesses, and those added costs increase the price we pay for goods and services. Notwithstanding the original predicate offense—such as drug dealing or arms trading—the results of money laundering affect everyone. Further, battling money launderers not only reduces financial crime but also diminishes the resources they have to commit other major crimes.

The Three Stages of Money Laundering

Learn it. Know it. Live it. The following concepts are the foundation to understanding money laundering. Any test you may ever take about this subject, or any certification that you might strive for, will almost always ask questions about the three stages of money laundering.

1. Placement

2. Layering

3. Integration

   Let's look at each one in turn.

Placement

Placement is the first stage of the process. Simply, this is the act of physically taking bulk cash proceeds and bringing them to a financial institution for deposit or transfer. That seems easy enough, right? Well, perhaps to the average person bringing cash to the bank is no big deal, but let me describe a unique problem that the bad guys have. That problem is size and weight. Keep in mind that your friendly neighborhood drug dealer does not usually accept American Express, MasterCard, or Visa. Personal checks are usually out as well, so that leaves either paper or digital forms of money (I'll discuss digital in Chapter 2.

   The street-corner drug dealer usually gets paid in paper money, in other words, singles, fives, tens, twenties, and, less frequently, hundreds. Earlier I talked about the height of a billion and a trillion dollars. Now let's discuss weight: 450 paper bills weigh 1 pound, so $1 million in $5 bills weigh 440 pounds, $1 million in $10 bills weigh 220 pounds, $1 million in $20 bills weigh 110 pounds, and $1 million in $100 bills weigh 22 pounds. Further, keep in mind that your friendly neighborhood drug dealer does not get paid often in $100 bills. He sees mostly singles, fives, tens, and twenties. Doing the math, you can see how quickly this can become an issue. It's hard to carry and move such a heavy load. Can you imagine some guy walking into the bank with a wheelbarrow loaded with cash? Do you think that just might be a tad suspicious? It certainly would attract a lot of attention from a financial institution. This is where the money launderer needs a good cover story—one that makes it seem all that cash appears to have come from a legitimate source.

The dirty money needs to be transformed into a less noticeable and more portable form and then "placed" into a legitimate financial institution. (Placed could mean the cash is deposited or substituted for another form, such as a money order, bank check, prepaid access card, and so on.) Since large amounts of cash can attract attention and may be subject to federal reporting requirements, criminals depend upon the use of businesses that deal with substantial amounts of cash. Businesses that might normally have large amounts of small-denomination bills include restaurants, bars, hotels, casinos, car washes, vending machine companies, and laundromats. The large amounts of cash can be broken up into smaller amounts that are then each deposited directly into a bank account, or else they purchase a succession of monetary instruments (money orders, cashier's checks, and so on) and then deposit them into accounts at various locations. The end result is that the original money has been changed and is one step removed from its original starting point.

The placement phase is the most vulnerable to detection by law enforcement. It is sometimes referred to as a "choke" point. As a result, law enforcement has concentrated on developing methods to make it harder to place ill-gotten gains without detection. Methods such as suspicious activity reports, currency transaction reports, and cross-border declaration rules (to be described in detailed later chapters) in all make it easier for law enforcement to recognize.

For example, Johnny Drug Dealer makes $50,000 per week selling cocaine in the Bronx. Johnny is sitting on approximately 20 pounds of small currency (singles, fives, tens, and twenties). Johnny Drug Dealer wants to get those ill-gotten gains into the system (placed). He can't just stroll down to the bank with a wheelbarrow full of cash, so he has to come up with a method that will make his cash appear legitimate so questions are not raised at the financial institution. The main concept to know in this phase is that the second the money passes from the bad guy's hands into a financial institution (bank, money service business [MSB], auto dealer, and so on), that is the placement of the funds.

Note
Proficient drug dealers usually keep separate locations, one for the drugs and

one for the money, and never the two shall meet. That's why it's called a *stash house*. The corporate term for that is *separation of duties*. Make no mistake about it, a major drug operation works much like a finely tuned corporation minus the murder and mayhem.

Layering

Layering is the second step of the three-step process. Layering requires the launderer to make numerous transactions, possibly involving several front companies and entities. By doing this, the launderer is attempting to distance himself from the money and make it harder for the authorities to track. Typically, these layers involve foreign countries that have strong bank secrecy rules, which in turn makes the cash trail harder to follow. It is to the advantage of the launderer to use as many layers as possible, using several shell corporations and moving numerous transactions through as many jurisdictions (especially outside of the United States) as possible. Other layering techniques involve the purchase of big-ticket items such as cars, boats, planes, or securities. These are usually registered in a nominee's name (someone other than the launderer); sometimes friends, family members, college students, and seniors are paid to be nominees. Casinos are often used to layer funds because they readily take cash in. Once converted to chips, the assets appear to be winnings.

Bank Secrecy Act One of the reasons launderers use countries with such strong bank secrecy rules is because of the U.S. adoption of the Bank Secrecy Act (BSA). In 1970 the United States passed the BSA, which required all U.S. banks to maintain appropriate bank records (for a minimum of five years) sufficient for a customer's account activity to be reconstructed. In addition, all cash transactions greater than $10,000 must be reported to the Treasury Department. It is done on a form called a currency transaction report (CTR). Last, all subjects transporting cash over $10,000 into or out of the United States are required to complete a report with the U.S. Customs Service. This form is called a currency or monetary instruments report (CMIR). The idea is to establish a paper trail so the authorities can trace the cash. Subsequently, many countries have adopted their own version of the BSA. On an international level, the Financial Action Task Force (FATF) is a leader in AML efforts on a global scale, and it has created the FATF 40 recommendation as a guideline so countries have an AML template to follow.

Why Layering Works

The usual answer you hear to the question "Why does laying work?" is that it causes confusion when investigators try to follow the money. To a certain extent, that is correct, but allow me to color that a little bit. First, every time funds are transferred, they might go to a different name or perhaps a corporate entity. Constant movement and name changing tends to muddy the trail. Second, when law enforcement "follows the money," it should be easy to follow the bread crumbs right to the front door of the bad guy's house, right?

Not quite. Law enforcement will start by sending a subpoena to a particular financial institution. The average wait time for a financial institution to gather all the supporting documentation and other information contained in the subpoena request is about four weeks. In that four-week time, the bad guy has moved the money, and perhaps he has moved it several times. So, when law enforcement receives the results of their subpoena and find out that the money moved from Bank A to Bank B, another subpoena is required. Guess what? That means it will be another four weeks until law enforcement finds out where the next funds transfer went to. Then, another subpoena, and so on, and so on.

A case might be going on for a year, and law enforcement still has no idea where the funds ended up. So, the concept for the bad guy is to keep moving the money around. However, the bad guy eventually wants to spend the cash and will stop moving it at some point. The idea for the bad guy is to move the money one more time than law enforcement is willing to follow. The game of cat and mouse begins!

Integration

The third and final phase of the money-laundering process is integration. This is the phase where the layered monies are incorporated into the legitimate financial world and assimilated with the assets of the legitimate system. In other words, it's spending day for the bad guy. This is the light at the end of the tunnel—the giant payday for the launderer. Finally, it's what he has been waiting for: the ability to buy cool stuff or do more bad deeds as a result of the proceeds of his crime. He will transfer the funds into the mainstream using various methods such as business investments, big-ticket luxury items, and real estate purchases.

Putting It All Together for a Payday

Here are examples of methods used in the three-step process of placement, layering, and integration: *Placement*

1.
The cash is deposited directly into a bank account or incorporated into the proceeds of a legitimate business.

2. The cash is exported out of the country.

3. The cash is used to purchase high-ticket items, goods, property, or business assets.

Layering

1. The money is wire transferred out of the country using shell companies.

2. The money is deposited into foreign banking systems.

3. A previously purchased high-ticket item or property is sold off.

Integration

1. Phony loan repayments or doctored invoices are used as concealment for the dirty money.

2. A complex web of wire transfers makes it difficult to trace the original source of the income.

3. The proceeds from sold goods or property appear to be legitimate.

Here is a case example revealing the three-step process: Johnny Drug Dealer generated $20,000 a week in the sale of ecstasy in a small, upstate New York college town. Johnny, who was unemployed, understood that he needed to show a form of income so as not to make himself appear suspicious to law enforcement. Johnny would follow the three methods of money laundering.

- *Placement*: Johnny needed to change the form of the money from ill-gotten cash gains into something that would be subtle.

- *Layering*: Johnny did not want to be tracked back to the origin of the cash.

- *Integration*: Johnny needed the cash to look as though it came from a legitimate source.

Johnny used a nominee (a person who is purported to be the legal owner of a business or account but in reality is just the owner in name only) and slowly funneled cash into his account. He structured his deposits (less than $10,000 each, for reasons covered in more detail later) until he had enough to purchase a pizza parlor in town. Hence, some of his dirty money has now been "placed." Johnny was also separated from the cash by using a nominee to be the owner. So, Johnny covered the layering process. Further, since Johnny now could show that he was employed, he could get credit from the bank to make purchases such as real estate.

Johnny's pizza business appeared to be a smashing success. Johnny was incorporating the dirty money along with the legitimate money from the pizza parlor. He was making cash deposits of approximately $3,000 a day. On paper, it appeared that Johnny's pizza parlor was doing great business, at least until law enforcement surveillance noted that Johnny's pizza shop did not seem to do a lot of business and $3,000 a day seemed a bit high. Law enforcement checked with the previous owner of the pizza shop who stated that he was lucky to make $500 a day, never mind $3,000. A review of his purchases for supplies (pizza dough, sauce, cheese, and so on) did not indicate the kind of demand $3,000 a day of sales would merit. Further investigation led to Johnny's arrest and the seizure of his assets. Of course, this is an elementary example, but it contains all the elements of money laundering.

Who Launders Money

Crimes are committed for one of four reasons. The first and probably accountable for 95 percent of most crime is greed/profit/personal gain, from the drug lord to the low-level street seller, from the master con man to the afternoon burglar, and from the corporate embezzler to the credit card skimmer. It's almost always about money!

The next reason for crime is passion, from a guy coming home to find his wife in bed with his next-door neighbor to two drunks in a bar duking it out. There is not much to gain here except revenge, ego, or pride. Such crimes are close to impossible to predict, and fortunately it does not account for much of a percentage of the overall crime picture.

The third reason is terrorism. Crimes that have terrorism at the core may be committed for the money, but the money supports the larger cause. In the efforts to support their cause, terrorists will attempt to intimidate and influence the policy of a government or civilians. But the cause needs financial support. Bullets and bombs cost money.

The last reason for crime is the unbalanced mind. Why does a guy walk into a movie theater or a school and start shooting up the place? This is much harder to predict and therefore much more difficult to defend.

The vast majority of the "for-profit" crimes—95 percent of the total number of crimes, remember—are committed by some form of organized, criminal enterprise. When people hear the term *organized crime*, they have a tendency to think of *The Godfather* or *The Sopranos*. What many people don't realize is that there are forms of the mafia in almost all ethnic groups, including the Russian mob, Italian mob, Irish mob, Jewish mob, Nigerian mob, Chinese mob, and so forth.

And there are lots of other forms of organized criminal enterprises: street gangs (Bloods, Crips, Latin Kings), outlaw motorcycle gangs, independent organizations, and terrorist groups (including domestic terrorist groups). There are a few independent criminals out there, but they are an inconsequential percentage of the total.

Don't get too depressed thinking about all the bad guys out there looking to separate you from your money. (Geez, I'm depressing myself. I may have to run out to church when I finish writing this chapter.) Fortunately, though, there are a lot of good people on the front lines fighting the battle against these criminals. They range from the military to law enforcement and regulators to all the good people working in anti-money laundering and fraud units in financial institutions. Each one plays an important role. Sometimes you might not think so because rarely do you see the case progress unless you are in law enforcement, but each part of an AML or fraud team is important. Working together is one of the best ways to put a dent in crime.

Summary

So, what have you learned so far? This chapter detailed the basic nomenclature of money laundering, how money laundering is accomplished, and why it's done. Further, the chapter reviewed the social implications of money laundering, detailed the three stages of money laundering, and noted just who launderers money.

These are the basic concepts that anyone entering the AML field should be aware of. Regardless if you are or will be working for a financial institution, are a regulator, or are in law enforcement, these concepts are the cornerstone of any AML program.

Footnotes

1 www.unodc.org/pdf/crime/a_res_55/res5525e.pdf .

2 *Smurfs*: The people who are used by money launderers to make transactions (usually deposits) below the reporting threshold of $10,000.

3 *Reshipper*: An intermediary who receives items and forwards them to another destination.

4 *Predicate crime*: To launder money, a previous crime must have taken place, such as gambling, drug dealing, or human trafficking. That crime is called the predicate crime. It is also known as a specified unlawful activity.

2. Methods of Money Laundering
How Do They Do the Voodoo That They Do

✉

(1)

When you get down to the nuts and bolts of laundering money, there are basically only three methods to move and clean dirty money.

- Using the legitimate financial system (for example, moving money through banks, MSBs,[1] and so on)
- Physically moving the money (for example, transporting bulk cash via shipments across the border)
- Physically moving goods through the trade system

In this chapter, I will describe some of the various methods of money laundering. This in no way is a complete list. Money laundering is constantly evolving, and new methods and techniques are always being developed. Every time the good guys build a 10-foot fence, the bad guys will construct an 11-foot ladder.

Each of the following sections is simply a "briefing" because each technique could be the subject of an entire chapter and perhaps even an entire book. This chapter is meant to provide you with a quick heads-up and, more importantly, to make you aware of the most important fact of all—anything of value can be laundered.

> **Note**
> Anything of value can be laundered.

Structuring

By far, the method of laundering money most reported on is *structuring*. A person "structures" financial transactions when that person, or his agent, conducts or attempts to conduct more than one currency transaction in one or more days by separating deposits into several smaller deposits of less than $10,000 each. The reason for a launderer to structure deposits is to avoid the Bank Secrecy Act (BSA), which requires financial institutions to report all cash transactions over $10,000.

For example, Johnny Drug Dealer has $100,000 cash in small denominations from the sale of MDMA. Johnny knows that if he deposits all his money into his Citibank account at one time, the $100,000 deposit will generate a report called a *currency transaction report* (CTR). That would not be a good thing for Johnny because law enforcement would take notice of his deposit and begin to investigate. The answer seems simple enough; he will have three of his employees—a steer man,[2] a lookout, and a delivery boy—each make four deposits of approximately $8,300 into Johnny's Citibank account at several different branches. The reporting requirement has thereby been bypassed, and Johnny has successfully "placed" the money into the financial network.

> **Note**
> Legend has it that during an investigation by the IRS in Florida in which agents were conducting surveillance on a structuring operation, one of the agents commented that several of the runners who were physically placing the money into the bank accounts looked like Smurfs from the TV cartoon. The name *smurfs* stuck and has been the unofficial nickname used to describe individuals who make a series of cash transactions to avoid the BSA requirements. Hence, the term *smurfing* has become synonymous with structuring.

Bulk Cash Smuggling

Firm financial reporting requirements for banks and other institutions have forced many launderers to find other ways to move their ill-gotten cash. Bulk cash smuggling is a successful and frequently used method to launder ill-gotten gains. Once the cash is offshore and in a country with a strict bank secrecy law, the process of layering begins.

Cash smuggling is exactly what it sounds like. It involves large sums of cash hidden on a person, in luggage, in cars or boats, or in cargo, to name a few options. The launderer or his agents will attempt to get U.S. currency past U.S. Customs and out of the country. In recent years, launderers have tried to hide it in automobile transmissions, phony television sets, battery chargers, electrical appliances, diaper boxes, and grocery goods. Cars with traps[3] are not only used to deliver drugs but also used to smuggle money across the border. The launderer will also attempt to use airline couriers, private planes, commercial vessels, and the U.S. Postal Service. Further, the cash might be converted into negotiable instruments such as money orders and traveler's checks and mailed to overseas banks.

Most recently, money launderers have made use of domestic wire transfers to move the bulk cash to a transfer point close to a national border. This is done to alleviate the possibility of the cash being detected by law enforcement as it travels the highways across the country, and it also saves much time. From there the money is then physically transported across the border.

For example, Johnny Drug Dealer hires Joe the Rag Man to drive a trapped-out conversion van from New York to Mexico. The traps are filled with approximately $300,000 of cash proceeds from a heroin deal with the Five Percenters street gang in Jersey City. The object is for Joe to get past the border and bypass the reporting requirement on a currency and monetary instrument report (CMIR). Joe the Rag Man then makes a U-turn and comes back into the United States, this time declaring all the cash as legitimate revenue. Joe will have all the "proper" paperwork to indicate that the $300,000 is from his business dealings as an architect with Vandalay Industries. Once he gets the proper forms from U.S. Customs, he is home free.

Gold

Gold is used as an alternative means of moving drug proceeds out of the country. Gold is purchased with illicit funds from gold refiners or wholesalers. The gold is then melted down and molded into the shape of various low-value objects such as nuts, bolts, a variety of auto parts or tools, and so on. The items are further disguised by being painted gray or silver. The disguised gold is then transported by courier or air cargo to Colombia, Venezuela, or Ecuador. The gold can be sold at any point, but it is typically held by the organization until the selling price is satisfactory.

Money Service Businesses

Money service businesses, including the U.S. Postal Service (USPS), Western Union–style money transmitters, issuers of traveler's checks or stored values, and others, are often used to move money from point A to point B. (Keep in mind, there is nothing wrong with these businesses. Much like a bank, they can be used by a bad guy to help accomplish his goals).

Money Orders

Money orders, many issued by financial institutions such as the U.S. Postal Service, Western Union, American Express, Travelers Express, and MoneyGram, are the most common forms of money transfers The use of the USPS money order has traditionally been one of the safest methods to smuggle bulk cash. The USPS is quite reliable and is protected by the U.S. Constitution's 4th Amendment, which prohibits warrantless searches. An advantage that money orders have over cash is that they can be purchased in higher denominations and, henceforth, weigh less, making them easier to smuggle. Further, in a weird twist of justice, if the money orders are lost or stolen, they can be replaced.

Money order agents are required to obtain a copy of the purchaser's identification if the purchase is in excess of $3,000, and they must maintain a file that may be reviewed by the IRS. (Of course, investigators face an additional problem: What exactly constitutes valid identification? Is the ID a blatant fraud, and is the agent part of the conspiracy?) The way that money order agents get around that requirement is twofold.

- The money orders are bought in blocks, ranging from approximately $1,500–$2,000 at any one location.
- The money orders are purchased by smurfs who will buy money orders from several different locations during the day or over several days. They will also purchase them in odd dollar amounts to give the illusion that they are being purchased to pay genuine bills.

Money Service Business

A money service business usually offers a wide array of services that can be used to launder money. Airline tickets and foreign currency exchanges are extensively used techniques. A money remitter's services, in the form of wire, fax, draft, check, or courier, exist expressly for the purpose of allowing people who are unable to use the traditional financial institutions a means to transfer money. The legitimate business consists of wiring small amounts of money that foreign nationals want to send to relatives in their homeland. Until recently, customer anonymity was a principal feature of these services.

Regulations Involving Money Service Businesses

Beginning on January 1, 2002, money transmitters, issuers of money orders and traveler's checks, and the U.S. Postal Service are required to report to the Department of the Treasury certain transactions that meet particular dollar thresholds. The reportable transactions include the following:

- Transactions involving funds derived from illegal activity
- Transactions structured to evade the reporting requirements
- Transactions that appear to serve no business or lawful purpose

The regulation includes two different dollar thresholds.

- For transactions conducted at a money service business, a $2,000 ceiling applies.
- For transactions conducted by issuers of money orders from a review of clearance records of orders sold or processed, a ceiling of $5,000 applies.

Wire Transfers

The most common system for transferring large sums of money all around the world is through bank wire transfers. A wire transfer is part of the layering process. The cash has already been "placed" in the bank, and now it is time to move it and begin a cycle of deception aimed at confusing law enforcement. In New York, approximately $1 trillion is transferred via wire every day, and approximately $2 trillion is transferred globally every day. Wire transfers are an essential part of the legitimate global business community. Wire transfers used by launderers are mostly used in conjunction with shell or nominee companies. The banks that hold the accounts of such companies are most often situated in countries that have strict bank privacy rules. Federal banking regulations state that a record of the wire transfer must be maintained for any transfer greater than $3,000.

Now you can understand how the laundry process works when you hear people talk about money going to an "offshore" bank or a Swiss account and being laundered. For example, drug money in New Jersey is structured (*smurfed*) into an account at the Bank of New York. Then the funds are wire transferred to a bank in the Philippines (or another country that might be on a watch list for money laundering). Thus, the money is difficult to track once it is in a non-U.S. account in a jurisdiction that may be a bank secrecy haven. Fictitious documentation from a shell corporation (an organization that does not engage in any real business but serves as a conduit for funds) is generated, and the money is then transferred back into the United States and, thereby, laundered.

While financial institutions are the origin and receiver of a wire transfer, the actual wire transfer is completed by one of two legitimate wiring systems and one messaging system.

- *The Clearing House Interbank Payment System (CHIPS)*: This is the main electronic funds transfer system in the United States. CHIPS handles approximately $1.5 trillion in transactions among its 52 banks in 23 countries every day. Ninety-five percent of all international transfers go by CHIPS wires, at a rate of 390,000 a day.

- *Fedwire*: Operated by the Federal Reserve, this is mainly a domestic electronic fund transfer system. Fedwire settles large transactions between financial institutions, enabling them to extend credit to each other and their customers. The daily average of funds transfers is approximately $2.7 trillion. Fedwire networks with all the banks of the Federal Reserve and approximately 10,000 financial institutions in the United States.

- *The Society for Worldwide Interbank Financial Telecommunications (SWIFT)*: A Belgium-based operation, SWIFT is an international message service that financial institutions use to send their messages. The system carries instructions for wire transfers between pairs of correspondent banks. SWIFT accommodates more than 10,000 financial institutions in 212 countries. SWIFT provides the proprietary communications platform, products, and services that allows its customers to connect and exchange financial information securely and reliable.

How a Wire Works

A person who wants to send a wire transfer provides the financial institutions with the name of a particular receiving financial institution and its specific assigned number, an International Bank Account Number (IBAN) or a Business Identifier Code (BIC). The financial institution sending the funds transmits a message—using either SWIFT if it's international or Fedwire if it is domestic—to the receiving financial institution. The message requests that the receiving financial institution pay out as per the wire instructions. The financial institutions involved must have a communal account with each other, or the payment must be sent to a bank with such an account, called a correspondent bank.

A SWIFT code is the system that allows a transaction to go to the appropriate receiving financial institution. SWIFT, in and of itself, does not transfer funds. However, it transfers information signifying the transfer of funds. Only those financial institutions that engage in wire transfers would require a SWIFT code.

Wire Travel Rules
All transmitting financial institutions must include and send the following:

- The name of the transmittor
- The account number of the transmittor
- The address of the transmitter
- The identity of the transmittor's financial institution
- The amount of the transmittal order
- The execution date of the transmittal order
- The identity of the recipient's financial institution

All receiving financial institutions must include the following:

- The name of the recipient
- The address of the recipient
- The account number of the recipient
- Any other specific identifier of the recipient

An intermediary financial institution must pass on all of the information it receives from a transmittor's financial institution or the preceding intermediary financial institution, but it has no general duty to retrieve information not provided by the transmittor's financial institution or the preceding intermediary financial institution.

Casinos

Money laundering through casinos is a valuable method of placing and layering ill-gotten gains. The ability to launder Chicago mob money was one of the reasons that Meyer Lansky first developed a casino in the middle of the Nevada desert. It should be noted that over the years, the U.S. government has done a judicious job of eliminating organized crime from owning casinos and banks. There are many anti-money laundering (AML) controls in place these days, and it is a constant battle of good vs. evil as newer digital technologies creep into the casino landscape. The same theory applies to fraud at the casino. It's a light saber fight between the Jedi knights and the dark side of the Force.

The technique of laundering money via a casino historically has been quite simple. While some of the mechanisms have changed, such as Ticket In and Ticket Out,[4] the bottom line is still the same: Buy in with dirty money (placement)—for example, purchase casino chips—and cash out for either larger denominations of cash or a casino check. If any questions arise about the origins of the player's money when he tries to deposit it in a bank or wire it out, he will say, "I won big at the tables at the casino." Further, consider that casinos provide a 24/7 operation that bad guys can try to abuse at their convenience. To add a little insult to injury, because of all the safety features and security at the casino, it has been reported that bad guys like to go to casinos because they provide a safe place for them to socialize.

Currently, any cash purchases of chips in amounts larger than $10,000 are subject to being reported to the IRS on a currency transaction report (;). Just to throw a curve ball at us, casinos in Nevada are exempt from this particular reporting requirement, yet they complete their own reports with the Nevada Gaming Commission. Part of the Nevada regulations are that cash purchases less than $10,000 are to be aggregated if they exceed $10,000 in the same gaming area within one gaming day (24 hours). In tribal casinos, the regulation is similar except the time frame is within one year.

For example, Johnny Drug Dealer takes a trip to Vegas with $100,000 in small bills that are the profits from his homemade hydroponics marijuana empire. Johnny understands that if he buys all his chips in the MGM Grand and cashes them all back in an hour later, he will be subject to filing a CTRC. Johnny thereby starts at one end of the Vegas Strip, buying $6,000 to $7,000 in chips at each hotel. He plays a few hands in different gaming areas of the casino (blackjack, craps, and slots) and then turns his chips back in with minimal loss. (We are assuming that he will lose some money; it would be adding insult to injury to the law-abiding tax payer if Johnny actually hit the jackpot at the tables.) Johnny makes his way down the Strip following the same routine until he has cleaned up all his cash. This is a page right out of the smurfing handbook.

Definitions

> CTRC stands for Currency Transaction Report for Casinos. It is also FinCEN Report 103. FinCEN is short for Financial Crimes Enforcement Network.

Historically, casinos were some of the methods of choice of organized crime to lauder their ill-gotten gains. However, casinos have come a long way to shoring up their AML programs. FinCEN has put out some nice information that details the red flags for abuse at the casino. Any casino workers, gaming commissions, regulators, or law enforcement would be wise to review the finer details on the FinCEN web site under the guidance for recognizing suspicious activity for casinos and card clubs.

Trade-Based Money Laundering

Trade-based money laundering is known as an *alternate remittance system*. According to the Financial Action Task Force (FATF), trade-based money laundering is defined as follows:

> *"The process of disguising the proceeds of crime and moving value through the use of trade transactions in an attempt to legitimize their illicit origins. In practice, this can be achieved through the misrepresentation of the price, quantity, or quality of imports or exports. Moreover, trade-based money laundering techniques vary in complexity and are frequently used in combination with other money laundering techniques to further obscure the money trail."* [5]

In other words, the bad guys change currency into products of value. (Anything of value can be laundered.) Then they can disguise the transactions as some form of trade. Much like the layering process referred to in Chapter 1, the launderer uses a complex network of businesses and documentation. The process is perpetrated by using phony invoices to make the product appear either higher or lower than the actual price.

There are three methods of trade-based money laundering.

- Over-and under-invoicing
- Black Market Peso Exchange
- Hawala

Over-and Under-Invoicing of Goods

The core of this particular method is the falsification of the actual price of the good or service in order to indicate a higher or lower value of the good or service between the importer and exporter. When a good or service is invoiced at a lower price than the good or service is actually worth, then the exporter is able to claim profit when the importer sells the same good or service for a much higher price, thereby indicating the funds came from a sales profit and not from ill-gotten gains.

In reverse, by invoicing the good or service at a price above the value of the good or service, the exporter is able to receive value from the importer because the payment for the good or service is higher than the value that the importer will receive when it is ultimately sold.

Here are some examples:

- *Over-and under-shipments of goods*: Mr. X has in his possession $1 million of drug proceeds. He goes to the auto auction and purchases 25 vehicles at $40,000 each, for a total of $1 million. Mr. X exports all the cars to an importer in Manila for the price of $10,000 each, and he has the fraudulent documents to indicate the volume and amount. Obviously, the exported price is much lower than the price he paid for the vehicles. However, the importer in Manila is working with Mr. X. As soon as the importer in Manila receives the cars, he sells them for the actual price of $40,000 each (plus a little something for himself). The Manila importer then deposits the "profit" into various accounts as directed by Mr. X. Mr. X has successfully laundered $30,000 on each vehicle.

- *Falsely described goods*: This technique (a subset of over-or under-invoicing) requires the misrepresentation of value or the quality of a particular product. Mr. X may purchase hard-to-determine value products such as fine art or antiques. Since the actual price is hard to determine, it is easier to doctor up phony paperwork indicating that the product is of a much higher or lower price than actual.

Black Market Peso Exchange

The Black Market Peso Exchange (BMPE) is one of the most widely used schemes for money laundering. Say a Colombian drug dealer has U.S. dollars in the United States as profit from his dealing. He needs to get the money to Colombia and in the form of Colombian pesos. The BMPE involves the purchase of U.S. products, primarily home appliances, consumer electronics, used auto parts, and other products for export to Colombia. A third party, commonly called a *money broker* or *exchanger,* takes charge of the process.

The exchange consists two separate parts—a Colombian peso exchange in Colombia and a U.S. dollar transaction in the United States. A Colombian drug dealer sells drug profit U.S. currency to a money broker in Colombia. The broker uses his U.S.-based contacts to place the U.S. currency into U.S. bank accounts while attempting to circumvent the U.S. Bank Secrecy Act (BSA) reporting requirements (applicable to deposits exceeding $10,000). The brokers then sell monetary instruments drawn on their bank accounts in the United States to Colombian importers who use these instruments to purchase foreign goods.

For example, the Colombian cartel arranges for the shipment of cocaine to New York. The drugs are sold to a major dealer in the Washington Heights section of Manhattan in exchange for U.S. currency. The cartel sells its U.S. dollars to a Black Market Peso Broker in New York. The money is sold at a rate that reflects the risk the broker undertakes of evading the BSA reporting requirements while placing the money into the U.S. banking system. When the dollars are delivered to the U.S.-based broker or his agent, pesos are then deposited into the account of the cartel in Columbia.

The broker then uses the laundered U.S. currency to sell to Colombian importers, who in turn purchase goods from the United States or elsewhere. Lastly, the goods are imported to Colombia and sold for Colombian pesos.

Underground Banking System (Hawala)

For those people who are unable to or unwilling to use the standard global financial institutions to move money, there is an answer. The underground banking system (also called the *parallel banking system*) is called by different names in various parts of the world. In Asia it is called Hawala. In India, it is called Hundi, and in the Far East, it is called fei ch'ien or the Chinese Underground Banking System (CUBS). It is totally unregulated and completely void of any reporting requirements. It is a system that operates outside of the traditional banking system of regulation and supervision. The system is inherently ethnic. You would not go to a Pakistan Hawaladar if you wanted to send money to someone located in Scotland. There are Hawaladars for most all ethnic groups. The whole operation is conducted on a cash basis, and a money trail is out of the question. Attempting to "follow the money" is virtually impossible without the use of a confidential informant.

For example, a Pakistan national decides to wire money from the United States to his homeland. (Note: It is common that this system would be used legitimately. One particular member of the Pakistan community in the United

States may collect money from all the members of the community. He then sends it back to one member of his family or community in Pakistan. There the money is divided up accordingly to all members of the community.) The Pakistan national contacts a member of the Hundi and gives him $10,000. The Hundi member contacts an associate in Islamabad and directs him to pay the equivalent of $10,000 (USD) minus a profit percentage to the receiver. Sooner or later, there will be someone in Pakistan who needs to send money to the United States, and the funds will already be here. No money actually has been transported across international lines. This is a simplified example, but it gives you an idea of how the system works.

Red-flag indicators of trade-based money laundering include the following:

- Transactions from unrelated third parties

- Unable to produce proper documentation

- Ghost shipments where no goods are traded and the documentation is fictitious

- Unusual shipping routes or product is shipped either to or from a high-risk country or through various jurisdictions for no known reason

- The use of shell companies

- Carousel transactions where the same product is repeatedly imported and exported

- Activity not consistent with the business

- Inconsistencies between the price of the product and the actual value

- Frequently amended transactions or extended letters of credit contrary to the normal business practice

---

Cyber Banking

Cyber banking is one of the newer methods of payment systems that provides for the electronic transfer of value. Cyber banking has the possibility to eradicate a money launderer's biggest nightmare, which is the actual physical movement of large sums of cash. Transfers of value are completed in one of two ways: Internet or prepaid cards. These systems provide new dilemmas for law enforcement because they have the capability to merge the speed of bank wire transfers with anonymity—a dangerous duo.

Smart Cards

A smart card is a credit card–sized plastic card that incorporates an implanted integrated circuit chip that can be programmed to accept, store, and send data. A smart card can be used to "load" money onto the card from a client's account from an automatic teller machine (ATM) or even a telephone. The cards store a dollar value, and the owner can redeem some of that value at a merchant location. Then the holder can "reload" it and use it some more. The smart card can hold approximately 80 times the data that the typical magnetic-strip credit card can handle. It is envisioned that someday smart cards will hold a person's medical records, driver's license, and other personnel identifiers. Further, they are capable of conducting person-to-person transactions, which would eliminate any third-party reporting agency. As of yet, this smart card technology has not taken off in the United States. The United States is still magnetic strip orientated, for the simple reason that it would cost a lot of money for everyone involved (financial institutions, merchants, and third-party processors) to change.

Internet

Cyber banks, which blossomed on the Internet, are not banks in the typical, traditional sense of the word. In fact, it is a good possibility that a cyber bank has no "brick-and-mortar" location. It exists only on the Internet and on someone's laptop computer. Most cyber banks are totally unregulated and unprotected. As a launderer, the positive side of this is that there are no reporting requirements and not much record keeping, virtually assuring your anonymity. The negative side is that there is no insurance, such as Federal Deposit Insurance Corporation (FDIC). If the bank should fold up and disappear, then so does your money. On the bright side, these cyber banks in the Unites States have all but folded up. It should be noted that online banking is not the same as cyber banking. Online banking is usually a legitimate financial institution with a form of drive-up window available via the Internet. There are only the usual AML concerns with online banking and, of course, any type of fraudulent hacking issue.

ATMs

Automatic teller machines are divided into two sectors, a bank-owned/operated machine and a privately owned/operated machine. A bank-owned ATM may be positioned as a drive-up/walk-up at your favorite bank. A bank-owned ATM may also be situated at an offsite location such as a mall or at the ballpark, but it is still maintained by the bank. A private ATM, also known as a private or white-label machine, can be purchased by an individual or entity and set up in any location (providing certain criteria are met by the various entities involved and ultimately a sponsoring financial institution).

What makes this work as a moneylaundering method is the confusion as to how the system actually works and being cognizant of the process to establish the beneficial ownership of the ATM. There are many entities involved in the process, including sponsoring financial institutions, third-party processors, independent service operators, networks, and cash vault management services, to name a few. In a quick moneylaundering nutshell, no ATM can be granted access to the "network" (for example, Cirrus, Plus) without a financial institution granting access. Therefore, the sponsoring financial institution must perform customer due diligence on the ATM owner. However, the ATM owner may sell or lease one or more of his ATMs to someone else who in turns sells or leases one or more of those ATMs to yet another individual. Due diligence is technically supposed to be performed on each owner/lease. However, the further removed the final owner/leasee is from the original owner, then the quality of the due diligence may suffer. The sponsoring bank may or may not be involved in the actual due diligence of someone who is three or more steps removed from the original owner. This is where one of the biggest issues come into play. If everyone in this process is on the up and up (as the vast majority are), then there are no problems because each successive owner/lease in the chain performs adequate due diligence on the person they are selling/leasing an ATM to. It is when due diligence is not performed or done poorly that beneficial ownership issues arise and the possibility of money laundering increases.

A launderer may purchase numerous white-label ATM machines and establish them in various locations. The places of business that the ATMs are placed in may or may not be a co-conspirator in the crime. The laundering bottom line is that the bad guy loads his ATMs with the cash proceeds from whatever criminal enterprise he is engaged in, or at the least, the money is comingled with clean cash. Subsequently, as cash in the ATM is withdrawn, the ATM is continually replenished by the launderer using his dirty money. Cash is withdrawn by unsuspecting cardholders who are making a legitimate use of the ATM, or cash is withdrawn by smurfs who are working for the criminal enterprise and making multiple withdrawals. The electronic transaction process debits the cardholder's account and credits the independent service operator's bank account. At the end of the month the independent service operator shows a genuine bank statement, which reveals money being electronically deposited into his account from a legitimate financial institution. Hence, the launderer has made his dirty money appear to be clean money.

The launderer had been facilitated by the fact that the privately owned ATM is several steps removed from the sponsoring financial institution. Until recently, they have not been in the heart of the radar zone for bank compliance and AML procedures. New federal regulations now require an AML program to be in place for the nonbank financial institutions that are involved with an ATM. There are guidelines for the independent service operator (ISO) to perform due diligence on the individual merchant, for the sponsoring financial institution to "know your customer" with reference to the ISO and/or merchant accounts, and for the networks to know who is using their systems. Until recent media attention, those guidelines were loosely maintained. Further hampering the system is the fact that the networks, processors, and ISOs are not considered financial institutions. Therefore, the Bank Secrecy Act, Money Laundering Control Act, Annunzio-Wylie Act, and the U.S. Patriot Act are applicable to them. The only regulated entity in the privately owned ATM transaction process is the sponsoring financial institution. Each time an ATM is resold or subleased, the due diligence process can get muddy because the accuracy and validity may come into question.

ATM red flags
Here are the red flags to watch for:

- The numbers of withdrawals from a particular machine exceed average for that location.

  - For example, an ATM in a small convenience store in a desolate location is doing just as many transactions as the ATM in a popular mall.

- The amounts of cash withdrawn from a particular machine exceed the average.

  - For example, all the transactions are at the withdrawal limit.

- The noticeable lack of any replenishment withdrawals. Follow the money trail. Where does the money come from that replenishes the ATM?

- Surcharges that are above average. The surcharge could be the payment back to the business owner for the use of his business to place the ATM there.

- The times of the day that the transaction occurred.

  - For example, is the location a local deli that is open only during the

---

day, yet many transactions are in the middle of the night when the location is closed? Also, note transactions at and around midnight —two transactions in a short span of time, like 11:58 p.m. and then a new day begins and another transaction at 12:01 a.m.

Prepaid Cards

The primary risk with prepaid access cards comes from the anonymity of the product and the ease of refining[6] and transporting value bypassing travel reporting reports. A person need not be a customer of a financial institution to obtain a prepaid access card; therefore, in most cases, identity verification checks are not conducted or are insufficient. People who do not or cannot obtain a traditional banking account can buy products and have access to ATMs via prepaid cards.

Remember, I am pointing out some of the risk factors of prepaid; it by no means is indicative of a bad product, because there are many good reasons to have a prepaid card. Much like credit cards or checks, they may have risks; however, the overall product is normally pretty good.

Prepaid cards were formerly referred to as *stored-value cards*. These cards are readily available in many retail establishments, and they come in two types.

- *Closed-loop card*: This card can be used only for the purchase of goods and/or services at a particular establishment (for example, Home Depot, Starbucks, or a mass transit card). They are totally anonymous.

- *Open-loop card*: This card can be used at a variety of different stores or could be a payroll card. The card may be funded by a bank account, which is less risky because the bank (assuming a U.S.-based bank) will conduct due diligence on its customer. However, the card may be funded by money orders or cash, which would be anonymous and have no trail to follow.

Within the open-loop/closed-loop realm, there are two subgroups.

- *Reloadable cards*: Maintaining possession of the same card, the owner can have value added to the card.

- *Nonreloadable cards*: The card is good only for the purchase amount of the card.

Open system cards may support anonymous cross-border transactions. Closed-loop system cards can be resold for cash. Prepaid cards have become one of the preferred methods of paying drug couriers by drug organizations. The major risk of the cards has been the ability to purchase the cards in the United States, load it up with drug proceeds, and then take out the cash in pesos in Colombia at an ATM.

The risk with prepaid comes in the form of anonymity and transportability. Anyone can buy numerous prepaid products without any retailer, or seller of the product, asking for any form of identification. There is no limit on the number of cards anyone can purchase. Hence, a bad guy could send out his team of minions and have them buy thousands of dollars of prepaid cards using ill-gotten gains without incident. Further, because the prepaid card is not considered monetary value, it is not subject to any reporting requirements as it leaves the country. Additionally, even if U.S. Immigration and Customs Enforcement (ICE) stopped a transporter at the border, it would be virtually impossible to ascertain the exact value on the cards. This makes prepaid access cards a viable moneylaundering method. It is not something that can move large sums of money quickly, like a large wire transfer; however, it is a method that the bad guy keeps in his bag of dirty tricks.

Autos

In many instances, autos are purchased as part of the integration phase of the money laundering process. However, autos are also purchased by the criminal enterprise as transport vehicles. Regardless, the vehicle is to be used by a drug mule or as a luxury car by the bad guys, and it may be purchased using cash, checks, and bank drafts. Because of some of the federal and state seizure laws, the criminals will sometimes avoid the ownership of the vehicle and choose to lease instead. Further, the criminals will make use of nominees to put the car in someone else's name.

Additionally, autos can be used exclusively to launder money. Vehicles are purchased for cash using illegally obtained funds and then sold overseas for double the price. In another scheme, an unscrupulous auto dealership may sell vehicles to criminals/launderers. The dealership, although required to complete a form 8300 (report of any cash transaction exceeding $10,000), will either disregard the requirement or complete the form with misleading information. The dealership may title the vehicle in the names of other individuals in order to disguise the trail of the transactions.

Correspondent Banking

A bank in one country (respondent bank) that has no banking presence in another country (for this example I will use the United States as the country with the correspondent bank). The respondent bank needs to have a presence in the United States to better serve its customers that must do business in the United States. For example, perhaps a U.S. company just began operations in a foreign country and the U.S. company had quite a number of personnel working at this new facility that required a U.S. bank to cash checks and make various payments. Since the foreign bank has no connection to the U.S., that bank would need some sort of financial connection to the U.S. A respondent bank will enter into a relationship with a U.S. bank (the correspondent bank). The correspondent bank performs due diligence procedures to make sure that the respondent bank has appropriate AML policies and procedures in place. The biggest risk of correspondent banking is the correspondent bank not knowing the actual person/entity who is the benefactor of the transaction. In other words, you don't know your customer's (respondent bank) customer (the respondent bank's customer).

Credit Cards

Credit cards could be used in the layering and integration stages of money laundering. On the bright side, the transactions are traceable. Further, usually there is a restriction on cash payments; in other words, the credit card bill can be paid for only by check. The risk with credit cards is the possibility of the money launderer prepaying his account to establish a credit balance. Then the launderer requests a refund. Of course, he receives the refund in the form of a check drawn on the bank's account.

Historically, there have not been many cases of money laundering by credit cards reported either by financial institutions or by law enforcement. This does not mean there are no cases, just that it is not one of the more popular methods, mostly because of the limited nature of amounts involved.

Real Estate

Laundering via real estate has become quite popular in the last few years, mostly because of the ease at which the laundering can be accomplished and the ability to fly under the government radar. In many cases, it is as simple as buying property using a unscrupulous appraiser who significantly lowers the appraised price of the property. The launder purchases the property via a bank loan for the deflated price and then makes payments using dirty money. Eventually the launderer sells the property for the actual value of the property.

Another popular method is using limited-liability companies (LLCs) to purchase property. Of course, the veil of the corporate structure comes into play.

The LLC is a good choice for tax evaders and money launderers because the true identity of the beneficial owner of the company may be hidden. An LLC can be owned by sub-LLCs, which in turn may be owned by sub-sub-LLCs, and so on, and so on. A puzzle can be created trying to establish the beneficial owner of the original LLC. In addition, an LLC can purchase and be the owner of real estate. In effect, some of the sub-sub-LLCs may send the laundered money to a number of the sub-LLCs that in turn send a check to the LLC at the top. This LLC purchases property using cash. Subsequently, the property is then legitimately sold, and the money has been laundered.

Cash-Intense Business

A *cash-intense business* is an actual storefront that deals in a certain amount of legitimate goods (a shell company or a front company may not have any brick or mortar). A cash-intense business is an enterprise that is almost predominately cash based (such as a bar, pizza shop, or car wash). The true ownership of the business may be cloudy because the business may have been purchased/registered to a nominee, particularly one who has a clean track record and would not arouse suspicion. Laundering cash through a cash-intense front means comingling the dirty funds with the legitimate funds. Because of the nature of a cash-intense business, it becomes difficult to determine exactly how much money the business actually made on any given date or dates. For example, the daily proceeds of a bar may come from selling booze. However, once dirty cash is comingled into the profits, it is easy for the bar to claim higher proceeds were earned. Without a detailed audit, it is difficult to determine where the legit and illegal funds begin or end. More profits could be explained in several ways—the drinks are more expensive, more customers are buying booze, bottom-shelf booze is being sold at top-shelf prices, there is a cover charge at the door, or perhaps there is a band fee. This complicates the true nature of the proceeds of the bar, and it becomes difficult to determine just how much money was actually made legitimately and how much was from ill-gotten gains.

The biggest red flag concerning cash-intense businesses is an unusual amount of profit that does not appear to be consistent with an entity in that particular line of business or inconsistent with that particular storefront.

It's all about flying below the radar (in most all of these methods). Knowing what triggers a closer inspection by financial institutions, regulators, or law enforcement is paramount to a moneylaundering operation.

Insurance

Certain insurance products can be used to launder money, particularly life insurance products. This is most often accomplished by using dirty funds in the form of checks, money orders, or wire transfers to purchase a life insurance policy and then cashing out the product prematurely. In the situation of using a general insurance policy, then fraud is added to the equation. The launderer would insure some high-priced goods and then make a fraudulent claim against the policy. In both circumstances, the end result is the launderer receiving a clean check that tends to legitimatize his funds being deposited into his bank account.

Some of the red flags might be the early termination of the policy and the refund check being directed to an apparent unrelated third party. Another method is, much like a credit card, over-funding the policy or borrowing the maximum amount available as soon as possible after purchasing the policy.

Digital Currencies

I'm sure many people believe that digital currency (also known as *virtual currency* or *crypto currency*)[7] will be the future of compensation-based finance. A more accurate description is a digital representation of value that can be stored or moved electronically. In the past, there have been several attempts by various digital companies to try to be the one digital currency that revamps the financial system. Unfortunately, they may have started out with guns-a-blazing, but many have fizzled out rather quickly. I am reluctant to mention the names of or detail the latest "world-changer" at the time of this writing only because it may be gone and forgotten about by the time someone picks up this book. Instead, I will simply focus on the method and not any one particular product.

There is one thing I know for sure; as soon as any new technology becomes available, there are bad guys out there salivating as they try to figure out how to manipulate the system, hoping to make an easy score.

Digital currency is purchased via a virtual currency exchange and then can be redeemed at any store that accepts digital currency as payment. The digital currency is maintained in what is referred to as an *electronic wallet*.[8] Unfortunately, digital currency is not regulated or insured by any entity. One of the major concerns is the anonymity of the accounts. Accounts can be created via the Internet, so any documentation is suspect.

The following are some things to be on the alert for:

- What is the safety and security of the e-wallet and transmission process on both sides of the transmission? Can it be hacked or victimized by cybercrime?

- What is the actual value of the unit of digital currency? Further, who decides how much it is worth, and what is the criteria?

- In the past, digital currencies have had issues with money launderers and criminal enterprises.

- The funds are not insured.

FinCEN has recently designated virtual currency exchanges as money service businesses, and as such, they are now mandated to have certain anti-money laundering policies and procedures. If digital currency is going to make it into the mainstream, it will have to follow the steps and procedures mandated by the Bank Secrecy Act.

Summary

This chapter briefly noted some of the more widely used moneylaundering methods. It is far from exhaustive, but it should provide a decent primer to those new to the industry and a refresher to those who have some experience.

The takeaway from this chapter should be that there are many different methods to launder money. Take solace in knowing that there are so many various methods it is difficult to know and completely understand each one. Take it slow and determine which methods might be used by one of your customers or, if you are in law enforcement, which methods your target may be using. Further, each time new technology is developed, you can be sure that there are bad guys out there trying to figure out a way to manipulate it. The only given thing in this industry is that crime won't be stopping anytime soon, and therefore there will always be the need to launder the proceeds of that crime. Therefore, there will always be the need for AML personnel.

Footnotes

1 *MSB*: Money service business—businesses that transmit or convert money.

2 *Steer man*: Used in street-level drug operations. This is someone who directs the drug-buying individual to the appropriate drug seller.

3 *Traps*: These are hidden compartments usually in vehicles or in a house. They are used to hide

contraband such as drugs or money. Sometimes these can be quite elaborate and controlled electronically.

4 *Ticket In and Ticket Out*: The modern technology now used by many slot machines. Instead of winnings being a coin payout, the winnings are digitized, and a winner receives a slip of paper containing a bar code that can in turn be redeemed.

5 FATF, www.fatf-gafi.org/topics/methodsandtrends/documents/trade-basedmoneylaundering.html .

6 *Refining*: Altering the shape and volume of the funds, such as turning lots of small denomination bills into fewer larger bills. In the case of prepaid, this means turning lots of bills into one plastic card.

7 Purists will advise you that there is a difference between digital and virtual currency. They consider virtual currency the domain of gamers who play various online games. They may not be wrong, however; value can still technically be laundered through the system, and that is the important thing to focus on, at least at this basic stage.

8 E-wallet is an encryption software that is used for all electronic commerce. An e-wallet holds a customer's payment information, and a "handshake" digital certificate is then used to store information, verify the customer, and access shipping information.

3. Federal Regulations

The Laws, Rules, and Guidelines Used to Fight the Good Fight

✉

(1)

We all enter the fight against money laundering so that we can deter, detect, and protect our financial system from the bad guys who would abuse and continue to perpetrate the predicate crimes that enable their illegal funds to develop. In other words, the bad guys are enabled to continue committing crimes because it is profitable. Part of the reason for profitability is the ability to launder the ill-gotten gains. So, we come full circle. The bad guy commits a crime, launders the proceeds, and then has the funding to commit more crimes. The drug cartel now has more money to push more drugs, buy more bullets, kill more people…and the cycle continues.

To fight the good fight, the United States (and other countries) has created guidance (often in the form of laws) to help prevent money laundering. The Bank Secrecy Act (BSA) mandates financial institutions to develop and maintain anti-money laundering (AML) programs. If you think back, Al Capone was arrested for tax evasion. Why? It was because he could not be arrested for money laundering because we had no money-laundering laws at that time. Fortunately, we now have many laws, rules, and regulations to assist in the fight against money laundering, which is, in reality, a fight against the bad guys who commit various heinous crimes. This chapter will briefly describe many of the legal tools in our AML tool kit.

1970: Bank Secrecy Act

The BSA requires banks and other financial institutions to maintain records to ensure that the details of financial transactions can be traced by investigators if they need to do so. Further, this regulation establishes economic guidelines for which reports are to be completed. Any cash transaction in excess of $10,000 has to be reported on a currency transaction report (CTR; IRS form 4789). In addition, anyone who physically transports currency and bearer instruments greater than $10,000 into or out of the United States is required to complete a report of international transportation of currency or monetary instruments (CMIR; U.S. Customs form 4790).

What Constitutes a Financial Institution

The BSA is clear about what it deems a financial institution. It is an agent, agency, branch, or office within the United States of any person doing business, whether or not on a regular basis or as an organized business concern, in one of the following capacities:

- Bank (except bank credit card systems)
- Broker or dealer in securities
- Money services business (MSB)
- Telegraph company
- Casino
- Card club
- Person subject to supervision by any state or federal bank supervisory authority
- Futures commission merchant (FCM)
- Introducing broker (IB) in commodities

Note
The USA PATRIOT Act, detailed later in the "2001: USA PATRIOT Act" section of this chapter expanded the definition of financial institutions and nonbank financial institutions.

Currency Transaction Report

A CTR, created by the Bank Secrecy Act, is a report that must be filed by a financial institution for a cash transaction of more than $10,000 in one business day. Multiple transactions must be treated as a single transaction (aggregated) if the financial institution has knowledge that they are by or on behalf of the same person and result in cash in or cash out totaling more than $10,000 in any one business day. An institution has 15 days from the date of transaction to file a CTR with the Financial Crimes Enforcement Network (FinCEN). Additionally, the CTR must be kept on file at the institution for a minimum of five years. Completing a CTR does not necessarily alleviate the need for a suspicious activity report (SAR); you'll learn more about SARs in the "1992: Annunzio-Wylie Act" section.

The following are transactions that require a CTR:

- Cash withdrawals

- Cash deposits

- Foreign currency exchange

- Check cashing paid in cash

- Cash payments

- Cash purchase of monetary instruments

- Automated teller machine (ATM) cash transactions (usually deposit only)

- Incoming or outgoing wire transactions paid in cash

> **Note**
> Check and wire transactions that do not involve the physical transfer of cash would not be considered currency transactions for CTR filing requirements.

Currency Transaction Exemptions

Exemptions to this requirement are extended to various entities that have applied for such exemption. Government agencies and other banks are exempt, for example. A business seeking an exemption would need to fill out a designation of exempt person form (U.S. Treasury form TD F 90-22.53), submit it to the financial institution, which then sends it to FinCEN. Businesses that routinely have large cash activities such as hotels or restaurants may apply for an exemption. FinCEN can provide guidance on those requirements.

Why a CTR Is Important to Law Enforcement

In many investigations or preludes to investigations, there is little information about a particular subject, entity, or target. An account holder might be clean as a whistle when the financial institution performs its original due diligence. However, the person who physically came into the branch (perhaps a worker bee, associate, or family member of the owner) to make a deposit/withdrawal may have quite the spectacular criminal history. When a CTR is completed by the financial institution, it might provide a lead as to who or what organization is behind that particular account. Sometimes solid leads come from the most unassuming of incidents.

United States to World Comparison: Currency Transaction Reporting

Many other countries requiring similar reports have a $15,000 minimum reporting requirement. In Europe, the EU Directive requires a 15,000 Euro minimum. There has been some outcry in the United States to raise the minimum standard because several financial institutions feel that $10,000 is too encompassing and cost prohibitive. To date there has been no significant movement by FinCEN to make any alteration to the minimum requirement.

Form 8300

Form 8300 is the nonfinancial institution version of a CTR. These also have a $10,000 threshold. An example would be a retail store that sells electronics. If a person bought $12,500 worth of TV and audio equipment and paid for it in cash, a form 8300 would be required. Historically, a money launderer might purchase high-ticket items with his new ill-gotten gains. Autos, boats, and electronics are extremely tempting for the bad guy. Fortunately, form 8300, which would subsequently be forwarded to FinCEN, makes it a little more difficult for the launderer to freely move his cash around.

> **Note**
> If you have a business in which some customers occasionally pay large amounts in cash for goods, you will need to fill out IRS form 8300 (www.irs.gov/pub/irs-pdf/f8300.pdf).

1986: Money Laundering Control Act

Launderers found ways to circumvent the Bank Secrecy Act, which led to the

Money Laundering Control Act (MLCA). One way to circumvent the BSA was to *structure* cash deposits (dividing up dirty money and making multiple cash transactions at numerous different banks all under the $10,000 report requirement limit). The MLCA made structuring a crime. The financial statute made it a crime for anyone to knowingly engage in a monetary transaction with criminally derived property of more than $10,000 with knowledge that the property came from unlawful activity (drug dealing, credit card fraud, counterfeiting, and so on) and is used in financial transactions to accomplish one of the following purposes:

- To further the criminal activity that generated the property
- To conceal or hide the ownership of the property obtained from the criminal activity
- To deliberately avoid a government-mandated transaction reporting requirement (CTR, for example) under state or federal law

---

1990: FinCEN

The Financial Crimes Enforcement Network was originally developed to assist law enforcement with investigations. Subsequently in 1994, FinCEN was given BSA regulatory responsibilities. The mission of FinCEN is to support law enforcement investigative efforts and foster interagency and global cooperation against domestic and international financial crimes and to provide U.S. policy makers with strategic analyses of domestic and worldwide trends and patterns. FinCEN works toward those ends through information collection, analysis, and sharing; technological assistance, and innovative, cost-effective implementation of the Bank Secrecy Act and other U.S. Treasury authorities (FinCEN, 2002).

1992: Annunzio-Wylie Act

The Annunzio-Wylie Anti-Money Laundering Act amended the Bank Secrecy Act. Financial institutions are now required to report any suspicious transactions that could be a violation of a law or regulation. The report that is completed by the financial institution is called a *suspicious activity report.*

To prevent financial institutions from any civil liability, a safe harbor provision was included. This enables the banks to report suspicious activity, through the use of a SAR, to law enforcement, without any legal repercussions. However, the disclosure of any information or even the existence of a SAR other than to appropriate law enforcement and regulating authority was deemed illegal. Further, Annunzio-Wylie made the operation of a money-transmitting business without a license a crime.

1994: Money Laundering Suppression Act

The Money Laundering Suppression Act (MLSA) of 1994 created a Bank Secrecy Act Advisory Group consisting of 30 individuals from the financial community who offer their advice and expertise in AML endeavors. The MLSA also eases the exemptions of transactions from the CTR reporting requirements. Numerous businesses that commonly deal with large sums of money on a daily basis, such as hotels, bars, restaurants, parking lots, convenience stores, and car washes, were not required to complete a CTR. While casinos normally deal with large sums of money on a daily basis, they were not exempt. In fact, the regulations increased with reference to the identification of players.

The regulation requires MSBs to register with the Department of the Treasury and at the state level. Further, it requires MSBs to establish and maintain a list of their agents. It became a federal crime to operate an unlicensed MSB.

1998: Money Laundering and Financial Crimes Strategy Act

The Money Laundering and Financial Crimes Act of 1998 designated certain high-risk geographical areas of the United States as high-intensity financial crime areas (HIFCAs). This was established to assist with the AML efforts of local, state, and federal law enforcement agencies.

There are seven HIFCA zones in the United States.

- New York
- South Florida
- Puerto Rico
- Chicago
- San Francisco
- Los Angeles
- Southwest Border

2001: USA PATRIOT Act

After the terrorist attacks on September 11, 2001, Congress enacted new anti-terrorism and AML legislation called the USA PATRIOT Act.[1] There are several sections of the USA PATRIOT Act. Those sections are as follows:

- Enhancing domestic security against terrorism
- Enhancing surveillance procedures
- International money-laundering abatement and anti-terrorist financing
- Protecting the border
- Removing obstacles to investigating terrorism
- Providing for victims of terrorism, public safety officers, and their families
- Increased information sharing and critical infrastructure protection
- Strengthening the criminal laws against terrorism
- Improved intelligence
- Miscellaneous

As you can see, the USA PATRIOT Act covers many unique areas. However, for the purpose of this book, you are specifically concerned with the areas involving money laundering. The act grants the U.S. Treasury the powers to deal with U.S. financial institutions for foreign money-laundering purposes.

The highlights of the legislation that this book is most concerned with are as follows:

- *Section 311*: Special measures for jurisdictions, financial institutions, or international transactions of primary money-laundering concern

  - Authorizes the Secretary of the Treasury to prohibit U.S. financial institutions from maintaining certain accounts for foreign banks if they involve foreign jurisdictions or institutions found to be of primary money-laundering concern.

- *Section 312*: Enhanced due diligence for correspondent accounts that are maintained by certain foreign banks

  - Requires U.S. financial institutions to perform due diligence and, in some cases, enhanced due diligence, with reference to correspondent accounts established or maintained for foreign financial institutions and private banking accounts established or maintained for non-U.S. persons.

- *Section 313*: Prohibition on U.S. correspondent accounts with foreign shell banks

- Banks and broker-dealers are prohibited from having correspondent accounts with any foreign bank that does not have a physical presence in any country (shell bank).

- *Section 314*: Cooperative efforts to deter money laundering

  - 314(a) allows for the sharing of information between financial institutions, law enforcement, and regulators with reference to possible terrorism or money laundering.

  - 314(b) permits financial institutions to share information, with reference to terrorism or money laundering, with each other.

- *Section 319*: Bank records and seizure of funds

  - 319(a) allows the U.S. government to seize accounts from a foreign bank if the foreign bank has an interbank account[2] with a correspondent bank in the United States.

  - 319(b) specifies a financial institution must reply to an information request, from a U.S. regulatory agency, with reference to one of its customers/accounts, within 120 hours of the request. Further, a foreign bank that maintains a correspondent account must maintain records identifying the owner and information about who is authorized to accept legal service for records surrounding the correspondent account.

- *Section 326*: Verification of identify

  - The adoption of minimal standards required for customer identification when opening an account. A financial institution must do the following in regard to new customers:

    - Get their name.
    - Get their address.
    - Get their date of birth (if the account is for an individual).
    - Get their identification number.
    - Verify their identity.
    - Maintain records of the information used to verify a person's identity.
    - Refer to lists of known or suspected terrorist or terrorist organizations generated by government agencies.

- The regulations should take into consideration situations, such as by mail or electronically, where the customer is not physically present at the financial institutions as well as the types of accounts and the types of identifying information that is available.

- *Section 352*: AML programs

  - Requires all financial institutions to establish AML programs. The AML program must include the following:

    - Developing internal policies, procedures, and controls
    - Designating a compliance officer
    - Maintaining an ongoing employee training program
    - Maintaining an independent audit function to test programs

---

Office of Foreign Assets and Control

The Office of Foreign Assets and Control (OFAC) is an agency of the U.S. Department of Treasury. The purpose of OFAC is to administer and enforce economic and trade sanctions against certain individuals, entities, vessels, aircraft, ports, foreign government agencies, and countries whose interests are considered to be at odds with U.S. policy. Additionally, the OFAC sanctions program targets terrorists, terrorist organizations, terrorist nations, drug traffickers, and those engaged in the proliferation of weapons of mass destruction.

For all you AML purists out there, technically OFAC is not part of the AML unit. Many larger financial institutions have a separate OFAC officer and unit. However, many of the responsibilities are so closely related to AML that it is often bound together with AML or at least works in conjunction with the AML unit.

OFAC publishes a list of individuals and entities that may be operating on behalf of a targeted county and subjects that might not be country specific. This list is known as the *specially designated nationals* (SDN) list.

Foreign Account Tax Compliance Act

The Foreign Account Tax Compliance Act (FATCA) is designed to combat tax evasion by U.S. taxpayers who have assets outside of the United States. FATCA requires foreign financial institutions (FFIs) to report to the Internal Revenue Service (IRS) information about financial accounts held by U.S. taxpayers or by foreign entities in which U.S. taxpayers hold a substantial ownership interest.

FATCA imposes new requirements on three primary groups.

- FFIs that maintain accounts for U.S. account holders or foreign entities substantially owned by U.S. individuals
- U.S. taxpayers holding specified financial assets outside of the United States
- U.S. financial institutions acting as withholding agents

Summary

The AML laws, as synopsized in this chapter, should provide you with adequate knowledge of the legal framework surrounding the fight against money laundering and the criminal enterprises that attempt to abuse financial institutions and our economic system. There are plenty of other guidelines, rules, and regulations that various regulating bodies have enacted. It would be advisable to stay abreast of the latest rules by frequently checking some of the following regulator and association web sites:

- FinCEN
- Office of the Controller of the Currency
- Federal Reserve
- OFAC
- FDIC
- SEC
- IRS
- State banking (each state has one)
- American Banking Association
- Association of Anti-Money Laundering Specialists

Next I will discuss how to create, build, and maintain a quality AML program. A financial institution puts all its AML knowledge to work as it attempts to construct an impregnable fortress to prevent money launderers from entering. (Realistically, no financial institution can prevent all money laundering. However, all financial institutions must make that attempt).

Footnotes

1 The USA PATRIOT Act is an acronym for Uniting and Strengthening America by Providing Appropriate Tools Required to Intercept and Obstruct Terrorism.

2 *Interbank account*: An account held by one financial institution (respondent bank) at another financial institution (correspondent bank) for the objective of facilitating customer transactions.

4. Building a Quality AML Program

For Financial Institutions

☒

(1)

The anti-money laundering (AML) universe basically consists of three entities that attempt to fight the good fight against the bad guys.

- Financial institutions (including designated nonfinancial institutions)
- Regulators
- Law enforcement

The AML unit of a financial institution is sometimes referred to as Compliance or Risk, or sometimes the AML unit falls under the auspices of the Compliance Unit. Its mission is to prevent and deter money laundering and terrorist financing. This is accomplished by creating and employing policies and procedures that implement the rules and regulations as set forth in the Bank Secrecy Act (in the United States).

In a nutshell, financial institutions take the laws developed by the lawmakers and the U.S. Treasury Department. They then follow established procedures that allow the regulators to maintain oversight, and they advise law enforcement of the required items. Sometimes the efforts of all three work smoothly and harmoniously, and money launderers are captured, criminal organizations are taken down, and everyone high-fives each other for a job well done.

Other times, there is a bit of a family feud. Financial institutions may object to what they perceive as too many regulations and contradicting oversight by their regulators. (Many financial institutions have more than one regulating body governing them).

Regulators sometimes have a different opinion and may even believe that there are not enough regulations. That would be evidenced by the fact that some financial institutions have issues maintaining a compliance program, and if it were not for the regulators, they would do little or nothing at all. One can somewhat understand their reluctance; AML is not an income-generating component of the institution. An AML unit can be quite expensive, and, in and of itself, there is no return on the investment. Hence, that alone is reason for some financial institutions to be hesitant to invest and develop a compliance unit any more than the bare minimum (if that even). Evading regulatory fines sometimes seems to be the only reason that some financial institutions will develop a compliance or AML unit. If you need evidence of that, you can look at a list of the latest regulatory actions. Don't stop after reading the name of the financial institution involved and the amount of the fine, but drill down to see what went wrong. However, that is looking at the money-laundering situation at a micro level. If you can visualize a bigger picture of where AML fits into the entire global economic system, then perhaps the view changes.

But let's get back to the nitty-gritty of some small financial institution that is only looking at the bottom-line dollar. The institution needs to be aware of a few important details that it might be overlooking. If you save a few dollars now by cutting corners on an AML program, then you may pay a hefty price later when the regulators perform an audit. Regulators might do the following:

- Fine your institution
- Force you to engage in an expensive look-back and independent review
- Impose remediation costs for repairing what the regulators say is broken
- Slap a cease-and-desist order on your institution that prevents you from doing business

Any one of those decisions will undoubtedly cost the financial institution a heavy financial penalty. Further, the stock or corporate value may go down. The reputational damage may seriously injure the institution. Quite possibly, some heads might roll at the institution. Keep in mind, these events are based only on the regulators finding deficiencies during an audit. Think about this issue. What if your financial institution is the conduit for the money flow that sponsors the next terrorist 9/11-style attack and it is discovered that your institution did little to prevent it or even cut corners to make a profit at the expense of thousands of dead and injured innocent people?

Bottom line
A quality AML program should be considered the cost of doing business, and

> it should be done to the best ability that you can.

The main function of the regulators (that is, FinCEN, the Office of the Comptroller of the Currency [OCC], state banking officials, or the Securities Exchange Commission [SEC], to name a few) is to make sure that financial institutions are compliant with the laws, rules, and regulations that have been set forth by the lawmakers. The regulators, after conducting a review of the financial institution's AML program, all too often conclude that the program is not sufficient, not being adhered to, or sometimes even blatantly disregarded. In those instances, the regulators will engage in a regulatory action that could include a fine and, in more severe cases, issue a cease-and-desist order or even rescind the financial institution's charter.

Fines can be quite severe, and they seem to be getting larger because it appears regulators have less patience for errors, omissions, or willful blindness. Rarely do we see the actual charge of willful blindness or financial executives going to jail. Most often there is a fine and a deferred prosecution. Many industry experts argue that as long as financial executives do not get prosecuted, then the incidents will continue. As long as the reward is worth the risk, someone will always take a chance.

Deferred prosecution An easy analogy is to think of a person who commits a crime. After he goes to court, the system may find him guilty, and the judge sentences him to probation. That means he gets a probation officer, and for a certain period of time he cannot run afoul of the law or he will be sent to the jail. Deferred prosecution means that the financial institution does not admit any wrongdoing; however, they agree to the terms of deferment. That might mean for a certain number of years the financial institution must complete a remediation process as set forth by the regulator, and it may fall under the realm of a monitor who reviews the financial institution's progress (similar to a probation officer).

Law enforcement walks a line between the financial institutions and the regulators. It is not law enforcement's position to create policy. However, on occasion, because of their "hands-on" and "on the front lines" duties, they sometimes do work with both financial institutions and regulators to advise them and make suggestions based upon what they see at the street level. This is particularly true whenever some new value-moving method is developed and implemented.

While there are numerous opportunities for all three parties to engage in conversation, usually through various seminars, workshops, and meetings, most interactions between financial institutions and law enforcement will come in the manner of subpoenas, SAR-supporting documentation, search warrants, national security letters, or treaties.

These descriptions constitute my "elevator speech" for describing the AML system as a whole. There is plenty of reading material for more in-depth discussion. Providing you with a basic working knowledge is the goal of this book.

Recommended Elements of a Quality AML Program

An AML program is constructed by each financial institution. No two programs will be the same because no two institutions are the same. JP Morgan Chase will have a different system than the local credit union or a mom-and-pop money service business. A broker/dealer will have a different program than a casino. While the scope and depth of the AML program might be different in various different institutions, they do all have to follow the laws, rules, and regulations as set forth in the Bank Secrecy Act.

There are three goals of a quality AML program.

- To prevent money laundering and terrorist financing
- To report suspicious activity
- To train all personnel on legal and internal procedures

The first goal, preventing money laundering and terrorist financing, could be considered the mission statement for any quality AML program. The biggest issue with this part is getting the financial institution to buy in to the reasoning. Everyone from the chief executive officer (CEO) to the newest teller should understand just how important the battle against money laundering is. Trying to convince an employee who may not be familiar with money laundering is the first step. It may be difficult for a person working at a financial institution who is not familiar with organized crime, or the criminal mind, to understand how or why this topic matters. After all, a fraud is easy to comprehend. An employee can see fraud, can understand fraud, and can see the financial loss. However, money laundering is not as visual. Where are the victims? The bank is not losing any money. Customers don't seem to have their accounts hijacked. So, convincing that employee why money laundering matters is the first hurdle.

Then, once the employee understands what money laundering is and who does it, it makes the rest of the program easier to sell.

Reporting suspicious activity is when the financial institution reviews the circumstances surrounding a particular account, transaction, or attempted transaction, and those circumstances are similar to known red flags for money laundering or the circumstances make little sense and are quite odd or unusual. A form called a *suspicious activity report* (SAR)—internationally known as a *suspicious transaction report* (STR)—details the incident and is forwarded to the government (FinCEN) for review. Because this is such a huge part of an AML program and one of the areas that regulators almost always recognize as an issue in any action against a financial institution, I will dedicate a section on SARs later in this book.

Training personnel is bit of a gray area because there are no specific standards for length and time of training. However, all personnel must be trained, usually on an annual basis. The length and constitution of the training methods are left up to each individual institution. All financial institutions must have regulatory oversight, and the regulator may determine that the financial institution's training program is lacking. Almost all regulatory actions against financial institutions note lack of training as one of the reasons for the action.

The Four Pillars

The generally accepted mantra of an AML compliance program is also set forth in section 352 of the USA PATRIOT Act in what is known as the four pillars of an AML program.

- Internal policies and procedures
- Designated compliance officer
- Independent audit function
- Training

Internal Policies and Procedures

If you were operating a retail business, you would develop your business structure and create a business plan. Similarly, that is what your internal policies and procedures represent for the AML program. These policies and procedures should include the risks that face the institution and detail how the institution plans on addressing those issues. This document should list all the components (inventory if this were a retail shop). It would include all of the financial institution's products, services provided, and geographical location. In general, the financial institution needs to establish the risks associated with the aforementioned services, products, and geography and develop a compliance program specifically designed for those risks.

The policy and procedures should notate how the financial institution will implement its risk-based[1] due diligence procedures. It should further establish just how it will monitor, analyze, and complete any specific transactions that would include suspicious activity and currency transactions reports and do so in a thorough and timely manner. Additionally, the policy and procedures should account for the supervision of its employees who fall under the auspices of the Bank Secrecy Act.

Account opening procedures should be detailed, and all associated customer information should be obtained and memorialized. The policy should also establish the guidelines for the "know your customer" (KYC) program.

The policy should detail how the financial institution plans to monitor for any odd, unusual, or suspicious activity. It should explain what circumstances would require "enhanced due diligence" and how those procedures would be implemented.

Every form and checklist that is created to complete the various requirements, such as KYC or EDD (enhanced due diligence),[2] should be noted.

The training program should be thoroughly described and detailed, and attendees should be noted.

Every regulation that your particular financial institution must be in compliance with should have a description of that regulation and a list of each of the requirements that you must meet (including any local laws for customers residing or doing business outside of the United States). Make sure that for every single requirement there is a corresponding policy that focuses on it. Essentially, the policy and procedures should discuss how your institution plans to complete the mission—avoid dealing with money launderers or terrorists—and then how your institution plans to perform a check-up (audit).

This must be in writing. Having all your policy and procedures in your head or on various pieces of scrap paper is not going to be good enough. It absolutely must be in writing and in some recognizable form. "Let's see your policies and procedures" is one of the first questions that your regulators will ask you when they arrive for an audit. Looking professional certainly is part of being professional.

It must be unique. No two policies are the same; each institution has different issues, concerns, and overall makeup. Having a policies manual that is customized for your institution and that meets all your requirements is the best idea.

The policies manual must be approved by the board of directors and noted in the board minutes. Note: When new senior management arrives on the scene of your institution, they should review the existing policies and procedures and sign off on them. It is not acceptable to have a policies and procedures manual that was last reviewed by senior management five years ago and two senior managers who are no longer with the institution.

In addition, you need to describe the procedures and circumstances for transaction monitoring, for alerts (trigger events), and for the closing of an account.

You can develop a risk matrix using a predetermined formula to determine the risk level of a customer (high, medium, or low).

The financial institution must address exactly how it plans to cooperate with law enforcement and handle the requests made by same.

All policies and procedures manuals should be reviewed and updated at least on a yearly basis. Special circumstances may require the policies and procedures to be updated even more frequently.

Software solutions

There are numerous software companies that produce an AML product. While they have many similarities, they are all quite different. Any software product should be adjustable to a specific institution and the products offered. For example, a software product and corresponding setup that might be good for a large global bank is probably not a good match for a small community bank.

I cannot provide guidance on any particular software purchase, but I can advise you to check out several different packages and inquire about the type of program and the amount of service provided by the manufacturer. (Remember, as regulations change, new laws are put into place, or new products are offered, the software must be adaptable and change along with it. Each institution's parameters will be different and need to be set accordingly and easily updated.)

Designated Compliance Officer

Every financial institution must have a designated compliance officer (DCO). The DCO, depending on the financial institution, may have other responsibilities. However, it must be a person in a responsible position and possess the capabilities to perform such a job. The DCO, anti-money laundering compliance officer (AMLCO), or money-laundering compliance officer (MLCO) is responsible for the daily compliance operations involving all anti-money laundering laws and regulations and the training program.

A DCO should be selected based upon the following guidelines:

- The designated compliance officer is appointed by the board of directors.

- The designated compliance officer must possess sufficient authority within the financial institution to accomplish the job.

- The designated compliance officer must be fully knowledgeable and experienced on the Bank Secrecy Act and financial institution activities.

- The designated compliance officer must report any Bank Secrecy Act issues and any SARS filed to the board of directors.

- The designated compliance officer must make sure that training and education are provided.

The money-laundering compliance officer First, the MLCO must design and develop the polices that are created to detect and deter money laundering and terrorist financing that are based on the institution's method of business. In other words, the type, size, and scope of the financial institution will be a major factor. A risk assessment of the institution's vulnerabilities should identify potential red flags of possible money laundering or terrorist financing. Policies should be created and adapted accordingly.

Second, there must be a policy on the enforcement and the supervision of the program. Consequently, there should be a procedure for updating rules, laws, and regulations or addressing new laws or procedures to address new risks as business operations change and/or new risks are identified.

Third, the training program must be addressed. A training program detailing how all appropriate employees will be trained is essential. Some of the issues to be addressed are the content and extent of each employee's training and/or retraining. Records of the training must be maintained. In addition, all employees should be trained in escalation procedures, in other words, what to do if certain red-flag activities are discovered. Additionally, a whistle-blower program should be established so that an employee can make a report anonymously and without fear of reprisal.

Independent Audit Function

It is not enough just to establish and maintain an AML compliance program. To properly evaluate its success, it must be appropriately monitored. A review of the program should be conducted internally by an individual or a unit that is not governed by the AMLCO. Additionally, an audit, commonly called a *review*, should be completed by a totally independent source or outside agency. Many of the large financial institutions use large accounting firms, such as one of the Big Four. Smaller institutions will usually employ smaller accounting firms, law firms, or private consulting firms. It is worth noting that almost every regulatory enforcement action taken against financial institutions observed that internal controls were weak or nonexistent. The main purpose of an audit is to make sure that the AML program is operating as it has been designed.

> **Note**
> It is not advisable to select a reviewing firm that is in lockstep with the institution. The concept is to have a fair and balanced review that might point out deficiencies in an AML program regardless of the financial institution/reviewer relationship. Many financial institutions choose to rotate reviewers each year.

The following items should therefore be considered when establishing or overhauling the independent audit function:

- The entire AML compliance program should be subject to an independent review every 12 to 18 months depending upon the institution's risk profile.

- Written risk assessment should be the first area to be audited.

- Qualified internal auditors, outside auditors, or consultants who are not responsible for the monitoring of the program should be used to perform the audit.

- Internal auditors should not be in the same management silo as the AML department.

The auditors should determine whether employees of the financial institution are using the procedures as required, verify that employees are being trained adequately, ascertain if appropriate records are being maintained, ensure that suspicious activity reports and currency transaction reports are filled out thoroughly and filed in a timely manner, confirm that high-risk accounts are reviewed regularly, and follow through on any recommendations made by the audit report.

Finally, memorialize everything. Be aware of the old saying usually attributed to regulators during an audit: "If you didn't write it down, you didn't do it."

Training

Now that you have established the first three of the four pillars of an AML program, communicating those plans to the employees is paramount. Setting up the best AML program in the world does you no good if the employees are not aware of or follow the program. That's why there's the need to establish a training regime. The following items should be considered when developing, overhauling, or reviewing your institution's training program:

- All employees must be trained, including senior management.

- The AML compliance officer must have the appropriate funds to provide training. (There's a gray area here. The meaning of the word *appropriate* may differ greatly depending upon who in the institution is defining it. However, the final determination will be delivered by the regulator. It may be a good idea to determine what a particular financial institution's regulator believes is sufficient for the scope of that institution by simply asking the regulator.)

- Training should be conducted annually and updated when appropriate. (There are always new laws, regulations, methods, policies, and examples that can be provided.)

- All employees need to be aware of the policies they specifically need to follow and how it affects their particular job. Having employees sign a document saying that they have read and understand the policies is a good idea.

- New hires should be trained immediately. Do not wait until the next training session. New hires need to be aware of the policies and procedures immediately, not when it is convenient to the institution's schedule.

- Document and memorialize the training.

FinCEN has not established a one-size-fits-all criteria because every institution is different and should be treated uniquely. For example, a small credit union with no overseas or international relationships may not require classes on cross-border transactions. Also, there is no set time frame on training. Each regulator will evaluate the training program based on the size and scope of the institution. For the sake of argument, let's just say that if you are one of the top 10 largest banks, a 20-minute webinar once a year is probably not going to make the grade.

The training program should consider the following elements:

- A history of money laundering, anti-money laundering, and terrorist financing

- A review of all pertinent AML laws and regulatory expectations

- Obligations of the financial institution to maintain compliance

- How to construct a SAR and how you get to the level of needing a SAR

- The consequences for an inability to abide by any of the rules

---

Quiz your students

Many industry folk like the idea of having a quiz at the end of the training session. This accomplishes three goals.

- The attendees are forced to pay attention (particularly after some type of web-based training, especially if the training is not interactive).

- It provides immediate feedback and can determine where the employees need the most improvement.

- It indicates to the regulators that the material is being taken seriously and provides evidence that the training program was provided and understood by the employees.

Finally, the financial institution should maintain all records pertaining to every training program provided to every employee (in-house or outside seminar attendance). Included in those records should be the training agenda (on a schedule if possible), when the training took place, all the materials and handouts, attendance records, and any quiz grades.

Risk Management

The AML program should reflect a risk-based model. In other words, the financial institution will direct its resources to the areas identified where the risk is the greatest. The financial institution is expected to identify the various risks that it is exposed to depending upon its products, customers, and geography and take appropriate actions to mitigate those risks and apply countermeasures. It is understood that there is no "all-purpose" method that will prove to be 100 percent effective. However, the financial institution must take reasonable measures to address and mitigate the risks identified.

The phrase *risk based* has been in use now for quite a number of years. Agencies such as FinCEN or the Financial Action Task Force (FATF) mention how an AML program should operate using a risk-based approach. It sure sounds pretty intriguing, but in actuality, it is just a way of identifying and labeling a particular subject, product, or transaction.

In the military, when things get dodgy, they might be at Def Con 4. Homeland Security in the days after 9/11 adopted a color system. You have heard the term *code blue,* and you understand that when you hear that in a hospital, then medical activities are performed at a higher level of intensity. What a "risk-based" approach means for a financial institution is that it should progress through their systems depending upon the level of the alert status.

Let's consider those levels, but first here's some background. A risk assessment is an analysis of potential threats and vulnerabilities to money laundering and terrorist financing to which a financial institution is exposed. The complexity of the risk assessment will depend on the nature, size, scope, and risk factors of the reporting entity. To accomplish this, a financial institution first must have a solid AML program in place as detailed earlier.

There are four stages of a risk-based approach to AML.

1. *Identification*: Identifying the AML risk to a specific financial institution and the general risks to all institutions. This can include either customer-related or issue-related risks.

2. *Analysis*: Understanding the risk. What is the financial institution's risk appetite? Is the risk high, medium, or low? The formula used to decide the level of risk should be included in the policies and procedures.

3. *Management*: Constructing and implementing the policies and procedures.

4. *Review*: Considering whether the arrangements are effective, whether they are being adhered to, whether the risks are being addressed, and whether they

could be improved.

To move into the risk-based realm, the financial institution might create a *risk matrix* or a simple checklist that can be used to categorize customers, transactions, and products. Performing adequate due diligence in each of these areas is paramount. Subsequently, each item would be provided a risk number or grade. Is a particular product high risk? Is the customer low risk? Is the geographical area that the transaction is going to or from high, medium, or low risk?

Table 4-1 shows an example of a risk matrix for a business customer. Note the considerations and categories. Where is the company located or conducting business? What type of banking product is being utilized? What is the construction of the company? (Sole proprietor? LLC?) What does the company produce? Table 4-2 shows the index used to score the risk.

Table 4-1. ACME Rocket-Powered Pogo Stick Company

	Dynamics	Ranking	Score	Emphasis
Country Risk	United States	Low	1	25%
Product Risk	Business Loan	Low	1	25%
Legal Entity	LLC	Medium	2	20%
Business Type	Toy Manufacture	Low	1	30%

Table 4-2. Index

Risk Level	Score
Low	1 to 1.50
Medium	1.51 to 2.25
High	2.25 to 3

Here is the computation: $(1 \times .25) + (1 \times .25) + (2 \times .30) + (1 \times .20) = 1.30$

The final result is that ACME Rocket-Powered Pogo Stick Company is a low-risk entity.

> **Note**
> Just because something is determined to be high risk does not mean you should not proceed. But it after reviewing all the variables, you still choose to proceed with a transaction or relationship, then you should be on high alert and monitor that account closely.

The Wolfsberg Group is an association of 11 global banks that create proposed industry standards for the financial sector including for KYC, AML, and counter terrorist financing policies.

According to the Wolfsberg Group, there are certain measures and controls that should be included in a risk plan.

- Increased awareness of higher-risk situations within business lines across the institution
- Increased levels of KYC or enhanced due diligence
- Escalation for approval of the establishment of an account or relationship
- Increased monitoring of transactions
- Increased levels of ongoing controls and reviews of relationships[3]

Essentially what the Wolfsberg Group is saying is that a financial institution must be aware of the various professions and industries that are historically at a higher risk for money laundering. A financial institution must know when to escalate matters to include enhanced due diligence and a thorough customer review. Additionally, Wolfsberg is suggesting a method for a heighted state of review for any high-risk entity or trigger event.

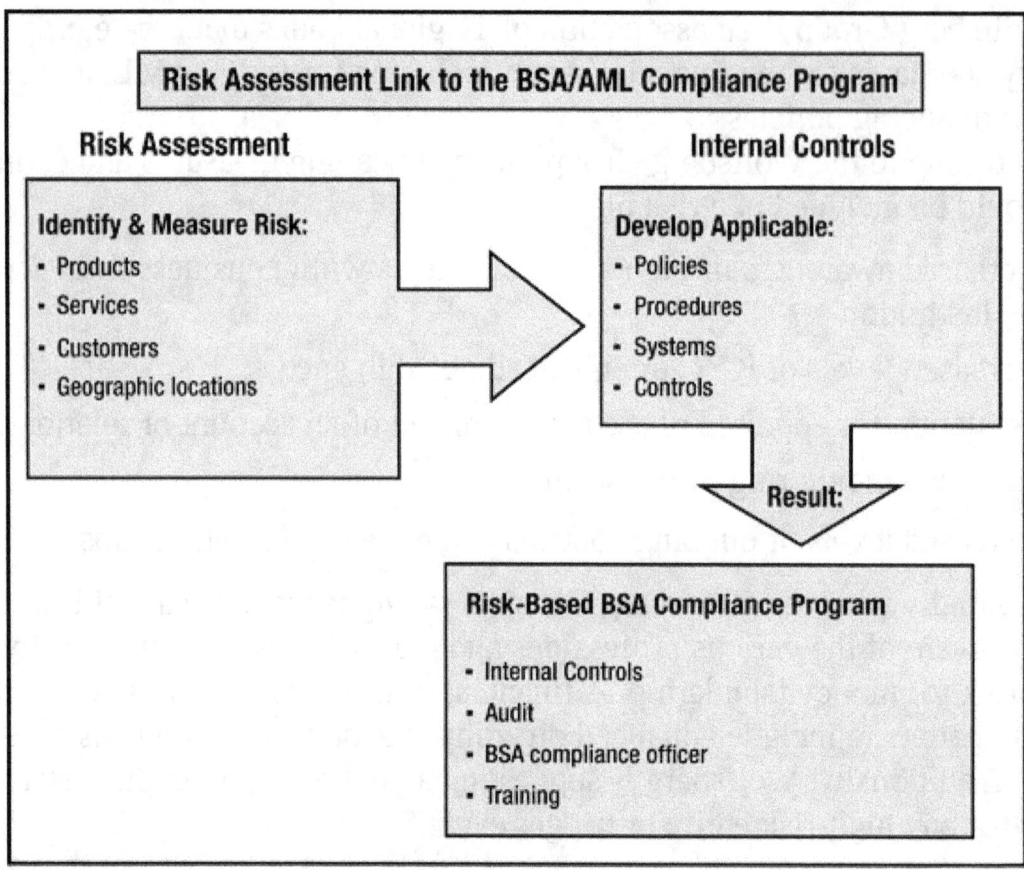

Figure 4-1. Chart from the FFIEC manual
https://www.ffiec.gov/bsa_aml_infobase/pages_manual/OLM_109.htm

Conducting Due Diligence

If you consider the four pillars as the foundation and framework of a quality AML program, then the meat and potatoes lie in its customer due diligence plan. There are three silos under the risk management concept.

- Customer risk
- Product and services risk
- Geographic risk

    Let's look at each in turn.

Customer Risk

Customer risk details and exemplifies each current customer and potential new customer by employing basic due diligence and enhanced due diligence criteria. In other words, the assessment of risk begins the second a customer first walks in the door (or first goes online) to open an account. The first step in the procedure is known as the *know your customer* program. Knowing your customer is quite possibly the chokepoint of the AML program and perhaps the single best method to prevent money launderers and terrorist financiers from abusing your financial institution. The ongoing review of the customer's financial proceedings and the transaction volume and number of accounts should be reviewed.

Consider the delivery methods of the product or services. The following are some classic higher-risk customer profiles:

- Foreign financial institutions
- Politically exposed persons (PEPS)[4]
- Foreign corporations
- Domestic shell companies[5]
- Cash-intensive businesses (such as bars, restaurants, car washes, and so on)

Once the financial institution properly identifies the customer and the business or product/services that it provides, then the formula for risk vs. reward may begin. Is the customer and their product so high risk that it is not worth the possible damage that could occur from banking a money launderer? What would make the risk worth accepting? Usually, the answer to that is money. The bottom line is, where does the financial institution draw the line? Each institution is different, and some may be able to justify accepting a higher-risk customer. However, they must be able to articulate that reason to the regulator, especially if issues do arise.

Product and Service Risk

Product and service risk comprises reviewing and analyzing the products and services that the customer is engaged with. It is also important to be cognizant of the products and services that the financial institution offers and understand how they can be used by money launderers. The financial institution should comprehend the potential risk posed by any new product or service. The following are some products that are considered a higher level of risk:

- Electronic funds transfers
- Private banking
- Trust services

- Foreign correspondent accounts
- Lending
- Trade finance

The underlying high-risk reasons for each of the previous products are many and can apply to various situations. The concept is for a financial institution to be well versed in its products and all the potential vulnerabilities that each product may present. This would be one of the categories in any risk matrix developed for a customer and, as such, part of a formula that will ultimately determine what risk category (high, medium or low) the customer would fall into, the amount of review that the customer receives, and if the account should be closed or not even opened in the first place.

Geographic Risk

Geographic risk is a consideration of the location. Is the business in an HIDTA[6] or HIFCA[7] area? Foreign? Does the product meet the expectations of the geography? For example, is your customer a business located in Miami, yet they are purchasing bulk loads of snowshoes? While there could be a reasonable explanation for that, until you verify it, you would find that circumstance a high risk. Generally, the following should be considered higher risk:

- Any OFAC[8]-sanctioned country
- Jurisdictions of primary money-laundering concern (as deemed by the U.S. Secretary of the Treasury, Department of State, or FATF)[9]
- Offshore financial center[10]

As part of the risk matrix formula, the location of the country of the customer or the country that the customer conducts business with is of major importance. First, if the country is under an OFAC sanction, then the financial institutions exposeure will be either nonexistent or limited based upon the type of sanction. Additionally, does the jurisdiction and its relationship to the customer's product and services make sense? All these are considerations for the institution's review.

Common Program Deficiencies

A review of numerous regulatory actions reveals that there are several common program deficiencies. Here's an analysis of some of those deficiencies:

- *Improper SAR filing procedures*: Some problems arise from downright negligence and some from lack of understanding. This includes everything from burying information to not picking up on what is truly suspicious. Additional reasons are a lack of enhanced due diligence, sometimes due to a lack of manpower, lack of qualified manpower, or a concerted effort to *not* find suspicious activity. (Quite frankly, lack of manpower can be applied to any and all of the program deficiencies.)

  Many SAR issues are simply due to an inability to properly complete the SAR form thoroughly or construct a proper narrative.

  Note: As I mentioned earlier in this book, when a person working at a financial institution does not truly comprehend money laundering/terrorist financing, the monitoring of alerts simply becomes a static chore of checking the right box on a form. When the staff understands and appreciates the scope of money laundering, that makes a huge difference. Further, the staff needs to feel that all their work is meaningful. In too many institutions, the staff rarely if ever knows that they have contributed in a positive way. Many people—and even institutions—believe that the SARS they write go into the black hole never to be seen again. Not so. Law enforcement looks at them, and there are SAR review teams around the country. They have proven valuable in numerous law enforcement investigations.

- *Weak customer identification program*: This starts right at the moment a customer walks into a financial institution. Without proper ID and truly knowing who the customer is, then all the following due diligence is moot. I will get into more details of this in Chapter 5.

- *Lack of suspicious transaction monitoring*: This stems more from a lack of proper parameters being set on an institution's automatic AML solutions software. In other words, the software is either picking up the wrong alerts or not picking them up at all. Further, it could be that the system is picking up on too many low-value alerts. Fine-tuning your solutions program should be a continuing item on the AML director's to-do list.

- *Inadequate policies and procedures*: Usually the policies and procedures just don't cover enough. Sometimes this is just an oversight. Sometimes this is because of new information, rules, or government notices that were never updated.

- *Lack of training*: This issue seems to always make it to the list on just about every regulatory action. Go figure. It's not difficult. It always seems to come down to budgetary concerns. Having a well-trained staff can alleviate so many problems down the road. However, it is difficult to prove a negative when trying to get a higher budget from the board of directors. What the board needs to comprehend is this: If you think training is expensive, try noncompliance.

- *The inability to identify high-risk customers*: This is an off-shoot of the customer identification/due diligence issue.

Summary

What you learned in this chapter is that developing, creating, and sustaining an effective and quality AML program is no easy matter. The goal of any AML program is to deter, detect, and protect. This is a process that begins at the moment a customer requests an account, and it continues until that account is closed. All along the way, various levels of due diligence are applied according to the level of risk that the customer presents. Many dynamics affect risk, and all must be considered and subsequently factored into some type of risk assessment system. The system is a living, breathing assessment because elements are constantly in flux and change routinely. The customer is under constant review (some more than others depending upon their risk level). A quality AML program is intensive work. The AML/compliance team is under pressure to make sure every stone is turned, yet the financial institution still has to turn a profit. Sometimes this can be quite the balancing act. However, the bottom line to note is that no shortcuts should ever be taken. While an individual financial institution may circumvent some AML measures to create profit, there is a whole lot of risk to the institution that goes along with that. Regulator fines are getting larger and larger. AML compliance officers are beginning to be held personally responsible. Media attention, especially if a terrorist event uses a particular financial institution, would be astronomical (let's not forget about any moral implications), and the reputational damage could be quite troubling. The bottom line is that the AML unit needs to perform well.

Footnotes

1 *Risk based*: Identifying the amount of risk and applying appropriate controls to mitigate the risk.

2   Enhanced due diligence – a deeper dive into the analysis and/or research then just the basic due diligence.

3   The Wolfsberg Group, "Wolfsberg Statement Guidance on a Risk Based Approach for Managing Money Laundering Risks," www.wolfsberg-principles.com/pdf/standards/Wolfsberg_RBA_Guidance: (2006).pdf.

4   *PEPS*: A current or former senior political figure, their immediate family, and their close associates.

5   *Domestic shell companies*: Business entities without active business or significant assets. The lack of transparency in the formation process can provide vulnerabilities.

6   *HIDTA*: High-intensity drug trafficking area—Provides resources to assist federal, state, local, and tribal agencies coordinate activities that address drug trafficking in specially designated areas of the country. Currently, there are 28 HIDTAs in the United States.

7   *HIFCA: High-intensity financial crimes area*—Concentrate law enforcement efforts at the federal, state, and local level to combat money laundering in designated high-intensity money-laundering zones. Currently, there are seven HIFCAs in the United States.

8   *OFAC: Office of Foreign Assets Control*—A unit of the U.S. Department of the Treasury. They administer and enforce economic and trade sanctions based on U.S. foreign policy and national security goals.

9   The lists are located at www.state.gov and at www.fatf-gafi.org .

10 *Offshore financial center*: Usually a small jurisdiction specializing in providing corporate and commercial services to nonresident companies.

5. Know Your Customer and Customer Identification Program
The Importance of KYC/CIP

✉

(1)

One of the first questions that I get from new jacks (new personnel) in the anti-money laundering (AML) industry is, "What is the difference between CIP and KYC?" The answer is that there is no difference. For the most part, the terms are used interchangeably. *Know your customer* (KYC) has been around for a while, and *customer identification program* (CIP) became common when it was mentioned in the USA PATRIOT Act. I have heard that CIP sounded less intrusive to the average customer than KYC, and that is why the term CIP was introduced. That sounds possible. (If not, it is a great line of baloney that someone came up with.) That being said, allow me to provide another point of view. Purists will provide you with this explanation: A CIP identifies the individual or entity that is attempting to establish an account or transact business with the financial institution. A KYC program takes that a step further and demands that you continuously have good intelligence about your customer, his source of income, his pattern of transactions, the products that the customer deals with, the geography of the customer, and those who he may be dealing with. In other words, the CIP allows the financial institution to know and understand who you are conducting business with and identify the customer at the start of the financial relationship. KYC allows the financial institution to understand that particular customer relationship throughout the life of the association between the financial institution and the customer.

Those are the correct definitions. However, the vast majority of people in the industry will use either term to describe the entire process.

KYC and CIP may be a bit befuddling, especially for financial beginners. It almost sounds like you are expected to be like the local bartender who knows all his customers and knows exactly what they drink and what sports they watch on TV. In essence, the bartender really does know his customer, especially when tips are part of the process. In the financial world, the banker is not expected to actually "know his customer" like a bartender. There will be no shouts of "Norm!" (going back a few years to *Cheers* humor) when a customer enters a bank. There are no high-fives, no cold icy brews sliding down the counter, and no local rock band playing their version of "Stairway to Heaven." (Now that I think of it, what a cool bank that would be. I think I'd much rather bank there than some stuffy old office filled with velvet ropes, elevator music, and waiting for the cattle call of "Next"…but I digress.) Perhaps in days long gone, employees of financial institutions may have actually known their customers, but today things are a bit different. There are so many customers, various branches, employees who move quickly to different positions, ATMs, and let's not forget online banking. To be fair to financial institutions, it is just about impossible to "know your customer" like the local bartender.

The true meaning of the current-day KYC/CIP terminology is to identify the customer, monitor his transactions, and update the customer's files according to the financial institution's policy. All of a customer's information is reviewed by various units within the financial institution depending upon the particular information. Sometimes information obtained can trigger a deeper dive into the customer or transaction. Other in-house units may become involved in a cascading effect. Whatever event triggered the additional in-house action can be cleared, can result in a suspicious activity report (discussed in the next chapter), or can result in a termination of the relationship with that customer (in other words, closing the account and not doing business with that customer).

Elements of a KYC Program

The first element of a KYC program is customer identification. The second element is the due diligence required to gather the information required. The third element is enhanced due diligence if the risk requires it. (By the way, I love these terms. Enhanced due diligence? What poor fellow was caught by his boss goofing off on the Internet one day and replied, "Wasting time? No, no, no. I am working on…um…er…um…enhanced due diligence…yeah, that's the ticket, enhanced due diligence." I've always wondered what would be the next term for the next level? Super diligence? Turbo diligence? Or, perhaps my personal preference, kick-ass and take-no-prisoners diligence.) OK, so I kid around about the terminology. However, I do understand the concept well. In a nutshell, you have your basic checks and your advanced background checks. I will discuss the "diligences" later in this chapter.

Customer Identification

The process of knowing your customer begins at the onset of the customer/financial institution relationship. The first day a potential new customer walks into or submits an online application to a financial institution is when the KYC process starts. The best place to prevent money laundering is at this beginning, the onboarding process. With some effective CIP jiu-jitsu, you just might save yourself a whole lot of trouble down the road. Regardless if the customer is an individual, corporation, private banking client, or correspondent relationship, the KYC starts at the onset of the relationship. Consequently, the KYC process is not finished once those initial forms are completed. KYC concepts should last for the lifetime of the relationship. As an individual or company moves, changes jobs, alters products, enters new partnerships, and so on, then the KYC must develop with it to maintain an up-to-date status.

Financial institutions, by law, must have a written CIP and incorporate it into its Bank Secrecy Act (BSA) policy and procedures that in turn are approved by the bank's board of directors. The financial institution should consider a risk assessment of the customer to consider the following:

- The types of accounts offered by the bank

> **Definition**
> An account is a formal banking relationship created to provide or engage in services, dealings, or other financial transactions including deposit account, transaction, credit account, safe box, cash management, custodian, or trust services.

- The bank's method of opening the account (in-person or online)
- The types of identifying information available
- The bank's size, location, and customer base, including the types of products and services used in different locations

The minimum responsibilities of any financial institution with reference to a customer identification program are as follows:

- Verify the identity of any person seeking to open an account to the extent that is reasonable.

- Maintain records of the information used to verify a person's identity.

- Maintain a description of the type of information it will obtain from the customer.

- Have procedures for verifying the identity of those customers to the extent that is reasonable and practicable and within a reasonable period of time before or after account opening.

- Have procedures for making and maintaining records related to the CIP.

- Have procedures for determining whether the prospective customer appears on any government list of known or suspected terrorists or terrorist organizations.

- Have procedures for providing notice to customers prior to account opening that additional information may be necessary to verify their identity.

- Have procedures detailing the actions the institution will take when it cannot adequately verify the identity of the prospective customer.

- Consult government lists of known or suspected terrorists or terrorist organizations.

Basic account-opening documents for individuals should contain the following information:

- Name
- Date of birth
- Address
- Identification number
  - For a U.S. person, a taxpayer identification number
  - For a non-U.S. person, one or more of the following: a taxpayer identification number, passport number and country of issuance, alien identification card number, or number and country of issuance of any other government-issued document evidencing nationality or residence and bearing a photograph or similar safeguard

Basic account-opening documents for domestic and foreign companies should contain the following information:

- Name
- Principal place of business, local office, or other physical location
- Identification number

Basic Customer Due Diligence

Customer due diligence (CDD) is essentially performing basic background checks of the customer, client, entity, or subject. (Any of those terms may apply). Enhanced due diligence (EDD) is a deeper dive to gather more intelligence about your particular customer.

A question that comes up a lot is this: "Does the financial institution have to verify the accuracy of all the identifying information that it is presented with?" The simple answer is no. However, the financial institution must verify enough information to reasonably believe that it knows the true identity of the customer.

Let's say you are a New York–based bank and a potential new customer presents a New York state driver's license, and the name and picture match the person sitting in front of you, I'd say that would be OK. If the driver's license presented is out of state and the picture looks like Alfred E. Neuman, I'd have to go with the "That's not good enough" response.

Each financial institution should have written procedures that establish the acceptable documents that they will allow for the CIP. The following are the usual primary documents (any one will do the job):

- State driver's license

- State ID card

- Passport

- Military ID card

- Resident alien card

Secondary documents, such as work IDs, health insurance cards, check stubs, and school records, should be determined based upon the type, size, and location of the institution involved. In addition, the financial institution should establish procedures for what they will do when they cannot identify the subject. For example, when the account cannot not be opened? Can the customer use the account until the ID can be verified? Should a suspicious activity report (SAR) be filed?

Account opening paperwork Can the financial institution keep copies of the account opening documents? Yes. For those who care, it is detailed under 31 C.F.R. 103.1221(b)(3)(i)(B). For both fraud and AML purposes, it sure does come in handy to have a copy of a driver's license or passport. As a law enforcement investigator, I was always happy when the financial institution had those items available when I subpoenaed an account. The only caveat is that the documents should be used only by the fraud or AML unit. The documents should never be forwarded to other units, such as a loan department or credit-granting unit.

Beware Shell Companies

Be wary of the possibility of a shell company. First, keep in mind that there is nothing illegal about a shell company. A shell company has legal status and renders few if any services or products. However, because of the limited amount of ownership-disclosure requirements, it can be an attractive venue for money launderers, terrorist financiers, or tax evaders. The use of enhanced due diligence techniques may be required to screen these entities appropriately. Many corporations have shell companies. Oftentimes it is for tax reasons. A simple red flag for a questionable shell company is to determine whether the shell company and its location, product, or service makes sense for the main corporation. For example, a major U.S. pharmaceutical corporation has a shell company that appears to produce portable igloos in the British Virgin Islands. Does that make sense to you? (Do not confuse shell companies with shell banks. Shell banks are illegal and have no legal presence in any country. Shell companies are perfectly legit) Further, be aware that bad guys will most certainly use counterfeit or forged documentation.This is a huge problem. All the due diligence in the world is useless if it is being conducted on a ghost or someone being impersonated. While no one expects you to be an FBI forensic document expert, it is incumbent upon the financial institution to form a reasonable belief that it has established the true identity of the subject.

Note
Record retention is important. All KYC/CIP records must be maintained for a period of no less than five years. That means you will need a formal procedure for retaining records and then destroying them—if you choose to— at a certain point in time after five years.

Identifying Customers Online

Online banking presents a unique set of problems. You typically won't have a face-to-face meeting to verify pictures of the person. For online account opening then, the financial institution should deem single-factor authentication techniques insufficient. The financial institution may consider the following:

- Requesting both primary and secondary documents for identification purposes.

- Requesting more than one identifying type of document and making independent contact with the subject.

- Making a phone call to one of the numbers the subject provided to verify the authenticity of the information. (I'd also verify the phone number via the phone book because anyone can provide a phone number and subsequently answer posing as a fictitious business. Call from a phone that won't provide caller ID information.)

- Verification of information cross-checked by the subject's credit report verifying documents sent along with a signed notarized form.

Monitor Transactions

In addition to account-opening procedures, monitoring transactions is an important aspect of a KYC/CIP program. The monitoring system mission is to detect any unusual activity relating to reviewing customer transaction information. A monitoring system is used to review all the activity, in real time, of all of the institution's customers. The monitoring system was created to assess the level of risk that may be associated with a particular transaction based upon preset factors that are calculated and set in the metrics of the monitoring software program that your institution has established. To monitor effectively, the financial institution has to know what is normal activity for a particular customer or other customers who have similar occupations and what is reasonable for that geographic area or type of product the customer may be associated with. In association with other risk factors, the monitoring system scrubs all transactions each day and notes those that appear to be out of the ordinary or unusual.

Also on the monitoring hit list is making sure that your financial institution has procedures in place for determining whether any new subject or transaction wire information appears on any government list of known or suspected terrorists, terrorist organizations, or any countries on the banned list. Many financial institutions have a separate Office of Foreign Asset Control (OFAC) unit or sanctions unit, but their results should be tied in to the AML team if any red flags appear. Usually institutions will use a third-party vendor that maintains the latest names on the OFAC list and any new sanctions or limited sanctions that might have recently developed. Be advised that dealing with OFAC.

OFAC list

OFAC maintains a free (and available to anyone) list of names, entities, and countries that have been designated as a specially designated national or sanctioned country or entity. The list can be cumbersome, which is why most financial institutions use a third-party vendor (that can be tied into their software). However, you can find the free list here: www.treasury.gov/about/organizational-structure/offices/Pages/Office-of-Foreign-Assets-Control.aspx

---

Many financial institutions have units specifically designated for transaction monitoring. Usually, when the institution's software detects a transaction that may be outside of the predetermined metrics for that customer, an alert is generated. It now becomes the job of the transaction-monitoring unit to clear or escalate that alert. The transaction-monitoring unit will use due diligence and enhanced due diligence to determine whether the transaction activity is of a risk that can be mitigated, and if so, it is cleared. If the alert appears to be something that could be considered suspicious, at that point the alert would be escalated. That means that a deeper dive or more thorough investigation of the transaction would be completed, and then a determination would be made on the status of the alert. The alert could be cleared upon investigation, all transactions from that customer could be marked for closer scrutiny, a suspicious activity report could be completed, or the relationship may be exited.

The Diligences

Many terminologies differ between the financial institution world and law enforcement. Having started my journey into the financial world via the law enforcement doorway, when I first heard the term *due diligence*, I had absolutely no idea what the heck it meant. I remember thinking the term *due diligence* sounded awfully impressive. I could imagine it on the front the bank's softball team jersey. When I finally figured out what a due diligence unit was, my first thought was, "Oh, a background investigation; now I get it." There was my first foray into the differences between financial institutions and law enforcement, with many more to come.

I did have a bit of a revelation at that time. I knew if I wanted to become successful as a government investigator in financial crimes, I had to learn the financial institution way. It began with terminology and acronyms (further complicated by the fact that each financial institution had their own acronyms). Then I tried to comprehend why financial institutions did things in a certain fashion and what they could and could not do according to the law and according to their individual policies and procedures. Finally, I tried to get a grasp on what, when, and how they could or could not provide information to law enforcement for the purposes of a law enforcement investigation. It was a lesson worth its weight in gold. The more I knew about how financial institutions operated, the more that helped me do my job. Similarly, the opposite can be true also. The more an AML investigator/analyst knows about what law enforcement usually requires and how the law enforcement–financial institution relationship works, the better they become at their job.

Due diligence
Usually this is the minimum investigative process that will satisfy the regulations. Note that this can be different from financial institution to financial institution depending upon the risk factor.

Enhanced due diligence A deeper investigative dive into the background of a person or entity. Usually this is because the customer may pose a higher risk of money laundering or it provides a higher degree of clarity of exactly who the customer is or the purpose of his transactions or the source of his funds.

Regardless of whether you use the terms *due diligence* and *enhanced due diligence, background check* and *deep background check, level 1 review, level 2 review*, or other terminology, the concepts are all the same. What you are trying to do here is gather a certain amount of intelligence on a particular subject. That subject could be a person, a company, a bank, or a country, to name a few. The physical process is all the same. Welcome to the world of investigations. I sometimes like to refer to it as desktop bounty hunting. The hunt is for information, and you are the hunter.

Start with a Checklist

The financial institution will most likely have some type of account-opening software that anyone who is authorized to begin a customer onboarding procedure will complete. That will contain the basic due diligence information. If a particular customer requires more work, it usually ends up on the desk of an investigator. (Depending upon the financial institution, there could be all sorts of various names of units. For smaller institutions, it is most likely work completed by a single investigative department.) It would be advisable to always begin the due diligence process by creating a checklist. The checklist would have a list of most of the usual sources of information that I would likely use during the hunt for information. This checklist would be either placed on the inside cover of the case file folder or, in a paperless world, simply placed in the digital folder. The checklist could be just an easily self-developed database-style list that indicates the source and the date. Check off each source, but remember that not all sources will be used, especially when just completing basic due diligence. Make sure to note the date that you checked this source. You should always note the date the source was reviewed. In the future, you may review the case file and note that it has been several months since a particular source was checked. It could be beneficial to rerun the check because new information may have been obtained since you last looked.

To give you an idea, I have created a simple starter investigative checklist (Figure 5-1). Under the header information, note the subject name, your name, the date the investigation began, and the case number. Then, come up with a simple checklist of all the sources to be reviewed.

Investigative Checklist

Subject	
Investigator	
Date	
Case #	

In- House Systems	Reviewed	Date	Misc

Commercial DB's	Reviewed	Date	Misc

Criminal History	Reviewed	Date	Misc

Internet	Reviewed	Date	Misc

3rd Party DB's	Reviewed	Date	Misc

Figure 5-1. A simple due diligence checklist

The checklist should stay with the case as part of your proof of due diligence. This helps maintain control over your case. Because as part of your job you may get hit with ten cases at a time and other assorted tasks, it's easy to forget what you have done and what you have not yet completed. A checklist is an easy one-stop shopping list of what has been done. Additionally, if another investigator has to adopt your case for whatever reason (out sick, on vacation, temporarily on another assignment, you got promoted, you got fired...whatever), then that investigator will be able to get quickly familiar with the production of the case.

Additionally, at a point in time where independent reviewers or regulators are looking over your cases, you will have documented everything that you have done in this case. Remember the old regulator adage: "If you didn't document it, you didn't do it!"

In your case folder (physical or digital), you will also have a copy of the results of each of your checks. For example, I would place the actual copy of the results from a Lexis-Nexis check in the folder. If there were no hits (results) from a particular check, you should take a screenshot of the page that indicates that there are no results and place that in the folder. When using a search engine like Google, you should take a screenshot of the first page of results. The page will indicate either no results or will say that there are 714 hits, for example. In either case, take a screenshot.

I understand that this may seem frivolous and time-consuming; however, there are two items that are of importance. One is that you do a quality investigation and relay your results appropriately. The second is that you are able to verify your work. Why is the verifying so important? Well, sorry to say, but in the past, there have been employees who fudged it. They said they did the due diligence, but they were either incompetent or lazy or both. When the crap hits the fan somewhere down the line and a customer of the financial institution turns out to be the next terrorist who blows up a building and the investigator who supposedly completed the due diligence turns out to have been lazy, the financial institution is going to take a big hit by the regulators and possibly by the media too. (Let's not even talk about the moral implications that you will have to live with.) You do not want to be that guy for so many reasons. So, this is why as a financial institution investigator, you must complete the due diligence thoroughly and then prove that you completed the job. In the end, it's not really a big deal to cut and paste or hit Print. It's just part of the success formula.

> **Tip**
> Have a mechanism to ensure enhanced due diligence has been done on a subject that you believe needs a deeper look. If something bad happens, someone will find out that the investigative process was either done well or, in some cases, not done at all. The results of that can be devastating.

When does it all end? When is enough enough? That is the $69,000 question. Sometimes when you latch onto an interesting case, it's easy to keep digging and digging and digging. Sometimes you will eventually find bones; other times you get zilch. I think getting excited about the digging is a good trait in an investigator. Look, poke around, overturn stones, shake trees, turn doorknobs…I love it. But, all things in moderation; you must remember that you do have other cases, and they will not stop coming in.

There is one thing that is a bit different in police work as opposed to financial institution work. In law enforcement, no one ever put a statistically driven number on the number of completed cases that must be turned in each day. Unfortunately, many financial institutions do set such goals, and I cannot say loud enough how wrong I believe this to be. I have seen financial institution adopt a position on the number of cases (alerts/lookbacks/reviews) that they want closed per day. This sort of puts a damper on the "How much should I dig?" question. I have seen people in charge at a financial institution who have never investigated a thing in their life (and I don't mean that to be insulting, just factual) telling seasoned, professional, retired law enforcement officers, FBI agents, IRS-CID agents, and others that they need to do x number of cases a day. Period. The quality and results were less important as long as the predetermined number of closures was met.

When the pushback from the seasoned pros began, so did the firings. The message was sent, do x or get fired. So, x it was. What may have been missed because quality and thorough investigations suffered is unknown. Apparently, people within the long chain of command in the financial institution made blanket statements to their bosses or regulators about statistics and workload numbers. Investigations are then averaged out to be x cases per day and y amount of minutes on each case. This may work for other aspects of a financial institution, but for fraud and AML, no way. Let me emphasize that again. No *bleeping* way!

A financial institution should be sure of its personnel's capability to do the job correctly, thoroughly, and completely. (In other words, hire talented people from the get-go.) It's tough to put a time clock on an investigation. Law enforcement never does. Did I get backed up while in law enforcement? Frequently. But, we always prioritized and got the job done. If there are that many cases at the financial institution, then instead of cutting corners to speed up case production, they should consider hiring a few more pros or some promising-looking talent who can be taught properly. Preferably instead of middle-level managers worrying about stats, they should "know their investigators." Understand what the investigators need and provide assistance to have them complete a thorough investigation. Perhaps the alert system in and of itself needs to be updated and the criteria for an alert reviewed. Any which way you spin it, putting time limits on cases is not a proper way to run an investigation.

Tip

Never put a time limit on any AML investigation. If so, the staff will cut corners—they really have no choice—and that may end up being a big mistake. Do you want to be the financial institution that banks the next terrorist group that kills a lot of people? The object of any investigation is to attempt to find an answer to a question, not to be satisfied by the fact that no answer was discovered in the 45 minutes allowed.

The irony of some of the incidents mentioned earlier has not escaped me. There are financial institutions that have already been ordered by their regulator to conduct a lookback. Why? They cut corners and didn't do what they were supposed to do originally. And lo and behold, here they are performing the lookback, and what are they doing yet again but cutting corners? Sometimes you just can't make this stuff up.

The bottom line is if you are going to investigate, then investigate without prejudice, predetermined outcomes, or any hindrances to the investigative process.

Beware of "Voo-Due" Diligence

A financial institution may choose to use an outside vendor to conduct its CIP and due diligence. There is nothing wrong with doing so. However, the onus is still on the original financial institution to make the right decision. If the hired hand screws up, it's on you. You and you alone are responsible. I refer to this type of situation as "voo-due diligence." When a financial institution contracts to use a third-party vendor for due diligence, you darn well better know exactly who it is that will be performing the services. Knowing who the CEO is does not cut it. I want to know who the people are performing the work. Are they low-paid analysts with zero experience in the field of investigations or financial crimes?

Here's a horror story on this topic. Years ago, when I was working in the major case squad just before my financial crime days began, we caught a homicide case. I will spare you the gory details of the murder. We captured the perpetrator within a few days, and for the purposes of building a solid case for the prosecutor, we began backtracking the killer's movements prior to the homicide. Our investigation revealed that the perpetrator was currently on probation and living in a halfway house. He had a job working at a call center. In fact, just about everyone working at this call center was on the rebound from some intimate tours of the correctional system. The call center had many different clients, including some banks, some department stores, and a slew of others in various industries. Did any of these companies inquire as to the background of the call center employees? Did these companies know exactly who they were contracting with? Apparently not. And the employees, some of the them hardened criminals, knew just what to do with the personal data and information they were required to ask.

By the way, some of the crimes that sent my perpetrator to prison before they allowed him out on probation were drugs and credit card fraud. Does anyone think it is a good idea to have a guy who is still on state-monitored probation time for committing credit card fraud to be currently working at a call center trying to hawk new credit cards to a list of potential customers? (To be fair, it should be noted that the homicide had nothing to do with anyone on the perp's call center list.) I know of financial institutions that have taken to farming out due diligence to Third World companies. Why? It's cheap. It's a cost-saving move. I don't know how that is going to play out yet. It does make the hair on the back of my neck stand up, but we'll see what happens as this runs its course. However, if history tells us anything, it is that every time a financial institution tries to cut corners on their AML, they suffer the consequences big time. Read any regulatory action, and you'll find this phrase: "Lack of a quality AML program." Is it any wonder? My final advice is that if a financial institution is going to use a third-party vendor to conduct its CIP or even its new-hire background checks, then the financial institution better know exactly who this vendor is and something about their reputation and their commitment to excellence.

When to Perform Due Diligence or Enhanced Due

Diligence

Due diligence will be part of the financial institution–customer relationship from the second someone wants to open an account to the day the account is closed. Without exception!

Obviously, upon application for an account, the investigative process begins. This may be started by some customer-facing employee (such as a teller or customer service rep) or a relationship manager or even a call center worker. Asking the right questions at this moment is paramount (each institution depending upon its demographics will have similar but different questions accordingly). Then that application will usually be vetted by the compliance unit depending upon where that customer/entity rates on that particular financial institution's risk matrix. If the customer/entity rates a low risk, then the investigation (due diligence) may be minimal. If the customer/entity is rated medium or high, then the level and thoroughness of the investigation will increase (enhanced due diligence.) Another time that the diligences will be rolled out could be if there is a material change in the customer's information, such as a new job or additional account holder.

Certainly if there is a trigger event, an investigation must commence. Then a determination must be made about the incident in question—is it something that can be mitigated, or should the account be closed? Regardless of the outcome, a written report will be generated. Depending upon the results of the investigation, a SAR may ultimately be generated.

Finally, regardless of trigger events or a material change in the account information, each account must be reviewed according to a predetermined schedule. The schedule is usually created depending upon the risk that the individual account poses. For example, a high-risk account should be reviewed annually. I suggest a review for a medium-risk account every two to three years and for a low-risk account every three to five years.

The Investigative Mind-Set

A bad guy thinks like a bad guy. He does bad-guy things. He acts like a bad guy. He spends his day trying to think up more bad-guy things to do. He associates with other bad guys who all do more bad-guy things and learn new bad-guy acts from each other. He goes to the annual Bad Guy Convention and Trade Show. He reads *Bad Guy Today* magazine. One of the advantages of being a bad guy is when a bad guy gets an idea, he can try it immediately. If it does not work, he can analyze, alter, and correct it and try it again tomorrow or try something completely different at any time of his choosing. He plays by no rules or regulations, nor does he follow any policies or procedures.

Team Good Guy, on the other hand, plays with an anvil around its neck. First, there is always the issue of the funding dilemma. I'm sure I don't have to remind anyone reading this book that prevention usually gets the last bite from the organizational apple. Further, there is the inherent issue that good people tend to think and act like good people. Most of us are not familiar with the bad-guy realm. Advantage Team Bad Guy!

The usual game plan for Team Good Guy is to fix all known problematic situations. Many times I have heard one of the good guys say something to the effect of, "We have policies that deal with that." Or, "We have top-of-the-line software," or "That has never happened before." However, while you may have policies against the usual suspects, transgressions, incursions, or any known issue, the problem manifests because it lies in the unknown or is a future issue that arises. The problem that you are not yet aware of is the most dangerous. Your criteria are effective only on known problems. And they are based on good-guy thinking. Just because the good guy cannot think of a problem issue does not mean that the bad guy has not or will not.

Trust Your Gut

It's important to use your instincts. Good instincts are part of developing the investigative mind-set. Your instincts come from your environment, experience, knowledge, and ability. We are not born with investigative instincts; they are developed. As I mentioned earlier, good people think like good people. This is why I sometimes bang my head against the desk when I read some of the AML blogs or listservs and it appears that certain people or entities being investigated are given the benefit of the doubt. Sometimes people even create excuses for them or their behavior by the people who are assigned the task of investigating them. Stop right there! It is not your job, nor mine, to determine guilt or innocence. It is our job to obtain the facts and report them.

When you don't have all the facts (and you usually don't), you make use of all your "instincts." While instincts have no place in the court of law, they should be front and center while you are completing an investigation. The more experience and knowledge you have, usually the greater your instincts. Follow your instincts, go through doors and open windows, turn over stones, but find as many of the facts as you can without predisposition or prejudice. If something does not feel right, then try to figure out why. Be suspicious yet judge slowly.

Here are some thoughts on developing your investigative mind:

- *Be suspicious, be suspicious, be suspicious*: Other than the usual account opening, a case has come across your desk for a reason. Somebody or some software has viewed this case as usual or odd. It is up to you, the investigator, to review, analyze, research, investigate, and then report. We all understand a person is innocent until proven guilty. That is for the court of law. Here's a news flash: This is not the court of law. I'm suspicious of everyone, at least until I can confidently cross them off my list. I cross them off by completing a thorough investigation, not by guessing, assuming, or being captivated by their nice smile. Remember, bad guys try to look and act like good guys. I'm sure there are some folk reading this who might feel that this is a terrible way to be. I'm not suggesting that you live your life suspicious of everyone all the time. I, for example, can turn it off anytime. Well…hmmm, OK, so maybe I don't. Bad example there. But you can turn if off when you leave the office. Being a replica of Aunt Bea from Mayberry (*The Andy Griffith Show*) is just not good enough if you want to be a top-of-the-line investigator. I mean, she could make a heck of an apple pie, but I don't think she'd do well tracking down terrorists. The job of investigators is to discover the facts as best they can. Each case should be approached with suspicion on the mind but with neutrality and evenhandedness as your course of action.

- *Implement the smell test*: If you think it stinks, it probably does. You do this job every day, and you work with people who do this job every day. If for some reason the hair on the back of your neck stands up, then go with the feeling. You are probably right. Understand, of course, that hair standing up on the back of your neck is not a valid probable cause in the court of law, so you do need to be able to articulate your feelings. What is making you feel this way? Figure that out and then run with it. This goes back to instincts. Don't be too quick to dismiss your gut feelings. If you can't figure it out, ask a new set of eyes to take a look. Don't be embarrassed to ask. I've been an investigator for decades, but I have yet to meet anyone who resembled Sherlock Holmes and had all the answers. We can all use a little assistance from time to time.

- *Consider multiple theories*: Understand one thing: If you consider only one hypothesis, you may be missing the boat. You must begin the case entertaining numerous possible hypotheses. The more knowledge you have about current trends and patterns, then the more hypotheses become available. Keeping up with and abreast of the latest and greatest techniques and methods is important.

Keep up with many new trends and patterns by bookmarking various web sites dedicated to money laundering and financial crime. Attend various seminars, workshops, webinars, and online training that are available. Belong to associations or groups dedicated to anti-money laundering. Join various groups on social media sites.

- *Make use of new sources of information or technology*: This might be more difficult because it usually involves spending budget money. However, there are other things that you can avail yourself of such as local meetings with your peers and law enforcement. There are also various free seminars, webinars, and trade magazines and publications. Don't forget general conversation with those in your department or area.

- Never say, "There has never been any cases before like this" or "No one has been arrested for this type of activity previously." Ahhh…the call of the mild! Hey gang, just because you don't know of any cases does not mean that law enforcement is not currently engaged in one or chomping at the bit to begin one. With new forms of technology (crypto-currency, for example) in the financial field, it is possible that there are no cases yet. That does not mean nothing is wrong and that you should bury your head in the sand. Did you ever notice whenever some nutcase goes on a shooting spree, the TV news interviews the neighbors and they almost always say the same thing? "He was such a nice guy; we never knew of any problems." You are not being paid to be the clueless neighbor—you are being paid to keep the place secure. Your job should be to envision the possibilities and create a path of action to prevent disaster.

- *Practice JADE (justify, articulate, and define everything)*: Assuming that you no longer have the Pollyanna "Everything is wonderful attitude" and have morphed into the "I'm suspicious of everything that moves attitude," then you need to follow the JADE rule. In an investigation, everything you do is memorialized. You never know where that file will end up; it could be the executive boardroom, a law enforcement facility, or a courtroom. You have to justify all your actions and further articulate and explain why you did what you did or why you did not do what you did not do. Your results will be defined, and ultimately an action will be taken.[1]

Perform Risk-Based Due Diligence

Risk based. Now there is a term that you will hear a lot. Essentially, when you begin the KYC process, you will be creating a financial profile of an individual, business, product, or geography. The depth to which you create the profile depends on the risk involved. The concept is that the resources of the financial institution should be steered in the direction of the greatest risks presented. This is similar to an analysis review in police work and what is referred to as COMPSTAT.[2] Essentially that is a Six Sigma–style statistical review of all angles of crime within a certain geographical area. The NYPD has used this method and is credited for the turnaround in NYC crime from the pits of the late 1970s to the thriving metropolis of today. There are four principles of the COMPSTAT process:

- Accurate and timely intelligence
- Rapid deployment of resources
- Effective tactics
- Relentless follow-up and assessment

Using that style of risk compliance has finally filtered its way to financial institutions. While financial institutions do not use the term COMPSTAT, a quality risk-based AML program mirrors the same principles. Once again, there are similar functions between public and private organizations, yet the names and titles are different.

Four types of risk are involved with financial institutions. They are as follows:

- Individual risk
- Business risk
- Geography risk
- Product risk

Individual risk is determined by the customers. Are they domestic or foreign? Is the account to be opened online or in person? What is their net worth? What do they do, and where do they do it? Do any red flags arise from the answers to these questions?

Business risk is reviewed by analyzing the type of business the subject is involved in. Is that type of business a known method for laundering money? What is the source of the funds? What type of banking will the subject be involved in? Does it make sense for the subject or the business? For example, one of the first questions that is asked during the application and onboarding process is, "What is the source of the funds?" So, does this make sense for the business the customer is engaged in? What if the customer states he is a fireman and reports that to be the source of his funds; however, he makes weekly large cash deposits (over $10,000). Or, the customer claims to be a local owner of a fruit market yet is frequently receiving large wire transfers from a gun manufacturer.

Geography risk is all about the location of where the funds are coming from and where they are going to, where the subject is, and where the account is. For example, a customer who's business is located at a ski resort and he reports to make various ski equipment is observed to be consistently withdrawing small amounts of cash from ATMs in Bogata.

Product risk is determined by what the subject reports regarding the company's output. For example, a fireman would have no product risk because he does not buy or sell goods. However, an importer/exporter would have risk depending on their product and the location it is going to or coming from. Would there be transactions from or to high-risk countries?

You will want to use a risk-review system like this both when accounts are first opened and upon transaction monitoring or other unique situations. Based upon the results of your due diligence, you will generate a risk rating that will determine whether the financial institution's customer, the product, or the location is high risk, low risk, or somewhere in between. A risk-based approach enables financial institutions to increase the return on their investment of manpower, funds, and resources that they put into their AML efforts.

Note
Many institutions develop a risk-rating matrix. They will come up with some type of rating methodology and assign a risk rating to that subject. For example, it might be as easy as High, Medium, or Low. Or it could be even more specific, such as High, Medium-High, Medium, Low-Medium, or Low. Or it could just be a number scale, 1 to 5 or perhaps 1 to 10. The risk ratings should marry up with the financial institution's BSA risk profile. It should be noted that risk ratings are not a one-time operation never to change again. Risk ratings should be reviewed periodically and modified accordingly.

In a financial profile, you are fashioning an image of a particular customer, client, or vendor by reviewing and analyzing items such as name, date of birth, address, incorporation papers, criminal history, negative news, sources of income, product, geography, and bills of lading—just to name a few. If the review passes muster, then the account/transaction is opened/completed. If there are one or two items that popped up during your due diligence, you must determine whether these discrepancies can be accounted for or mitigated.

In other words, here is where you begin a risk matrix. Compare the pros and cons of your customer, his transaction, or both. Can his transaction be explained? Does the transaction make little sense? Here's a simplified example. Say a customer is known to you as a buyer for a local health food store in Cleveland. Say she is suddenly depositing the $100,000 in proceeds from a sale of a truckload of snowshoes to a jewelry store in Bora Bora. Let's do a financial profile.

- The customer is a buyer for a health food store in Cleveland. What does that have to do with snowshoes, jewelry, or Bora Bora?
- Why would any store in tropical Bora Bora require snowshoes?
- Why would a jewelry store need snowshoes?
- Where did the snowshoes come from?
- Is Bora Bora on any sanction list or does it have a country risk rating available for review?
- Can you obtain any intelligence on the particular jewelry store involved?
- Review the customer's previous transactions for the past few years. Has she ever done this type of activity before?

You discover the customer has never made more than a $50,000 deposit previously (not that you need any additional red flags in this case).

In the risk matrix, you review all your facts and intelligence and then place a risk value on the event. Without some type of sufficient explanation of the previous activities, I would think that this would get a pretty high-risk rating, perhaps so much so that any transaction would be refused.

How much due diligence should you do to complete a risk matrix for an average account opening? The answer to that, unfortunately, lies within a great gray fog that can sometimes be as thick as pea soup. There is no definitive answer to that question. There is no regulating authority that will offer any specifics to guide you. The only thing you have to go on is that you need to feel comfortable that you did enough and that you know who your customer is. Further, you may need to explain why you feel that way to your regulator, so make sure you can elaborate on all your decisions.

Sample risk matrix

Factors	Assessment	Score	Percentage
Country/jurisdiction	Medium Risk	2	30 percent
Products/services	Correspondent	3	20 percent
Legal structure	Full Transparency	1	25 percent
Business type	High Risk	3	25 percent

The formula in this example is to assess the risk level (low, medium, or high) based on the following four factors:

- *Country/jurisdiction*: Where does the customer conduct business? Is it in a high-risk geographical area?

- *Products/services*: What type of customer is he? Private banking? Global markets? Retail business?

- *Legal structure*: Is the customer entity a corporation? Is the business on a recognized stock exchange? Is the business a partnership or sole proprietor?

- *Business type*: What is the actual description of the customers occupation, and what is his business? Is he an astronaut? A jeweler? An accountant?

An associated score of 1 to 3 is assigned (1 is low risk, 2 is medium risk, and 3 is high risk). The weight of the category is a percentage of the total. Following that theory, the categories of Geography, Products, Structure, and Business Type will each reveal a score (from 1 to 3), and then factoring in the percentage of each score will be the risk level of the particular customer. A score of 1.5 would indicate a low to medium risk. More categories can be added or altered depending upon your institution and its customers.

Sources of Intelligence

Sources of intelligence are the items that good investigators use to identify and verify facts. While all cases are different, for the most part it should be common to tick off boxes on the checklist of sources. When you get a hit regarding one of the sources on your checklist, then you should note the results exactly. You may need that information further down the line if you have to complete a SAR or document your findings in some type of investigative journal.

Here I will list a few common sources of intelligence for financial institutions. I will not go into long detail about each because I am not qualified enough to thoroughly explain how and why each of these things work. However, there are plenty of books and courses that will detail that for you. My goal is to simply make you aware of the possibilities. I will point you to the road. It's up to you to walk down the path. Here's the list, with more detailed explanations to follow:

- In-house systems
- Commercial databases
- Open source Information
- Invisible web
- Public records
- Social networks
- FinCEN 314b
- Specialized vendor databases

Let's fill in some of the blanks.

In-house systems. Check your own institution's resources across all business lines to look for any previous entries. Don't just check the name, but drop in phone numbers, addresses, and any other pedigree information you have available. Fraudsters and money launderers can be creatures of habit and will use the same names, addresses, post-office boxes, and so on.

Commercial databases. There are many such services available. Perhaps the most well-known is Lexis-Nexis. These are available via the Internet on a subscription basis. They contain a plethora of information about such things as people, businesses, addresses, and so on. It may tell you where your subject lives, including how long, who else resides there, and who owns the property, as well as convictions, licenses, UCC filings, or negative news, just to name a few. The amount of information is constantly being updated and added to. Having access to at least one commercial aggregator database is worth its weight in gold. The one caveat is that not all the information is 100 percent accurate. So, don't take a customer out back and waterboard his sorry butt simply based on some information from a commercial database. Verify what you can and use your head. These tools are all simply building blocks for your case.

Open source information. Learning how to properly use the Internet and the various search engines available to you is something worth investing your time in. I highly recommend taking some type of "How to Investigate Using the Internet"[3] course. What you currently don't know about Internet investigations will shock you. Locating the correct web site or tool to help you find answers or employing some type of analytics can be an enormous benefit to any investigation.

I will lump the concept of negative news into the open source category for now since unless you use specific third-party software, you'll be conducting your own negative news search. Negative news is just that. You scour the Internet to see whether your subject (or any related subjects) shows up in the media. You won't mind if he shows up as a war hero winning the Congressional Medal of Honor, for example, but if there is a recent picture of him doing the "perp walk," in handcuffs for embezzlement, then that is something that should get your attention.

The negative event need not be an arrest of your subject. It could be a story of a former partner who has been identified as a capo in the Genovese crime family. That in and of itself may be meaningless, however; keep in mind that you are in the building blocks mode. One item may mean nothing, but another three, four, or five items and your building blocks are starting to resemble a wall. It may not be up to you to make any decisions about exiting a customer relationship, but it is your job to be as complete and thorough with as much information as possible for someone to make that decision.

Invisible Web. This is actually much larger than the World Wide Web. The invisible Web is not indexed by the usual search engines such as Google; therefore, much information is hidden from view by the normal search engine portals. Much of that hidden information is in the form of various databases that are inaccessible to the way normal search engines perform a search. That is about as technical as I intend to get (or can get) with the reasons why; you'll just have to take my word that this is a great source of intelligence. Just to give you an idea of some of the intel available via the invisible Web, the following are some items you can look up:

- Archived web pages
- Blogs
- Business search engines
- Charitable organizations
- Intellectual property
- Newspapers
- Public records

The bottom line here is that much like learning about better basic Internet searching techniques, making yourself knowledgeable about the invisible Web will pay off in spades while you are performing your due diligence or enhanced due diligence. You can find an entrance portal to the invisible Web by typing **invisible web portal** into your search engine.

> **Note**
> When doing an investigation on the Internet, add *invisible web portal* to the search terms, and you will enhance the results you get, sometimes dramatically so.

Public records. These are records of various actions that are filled or recorded with a governmental agency. Examples are researching deeds and mortgages. The only downside is that there are still quite a number of municipalities that have not as of yet computerized their files and as such they are not available online. In that case, it's off to the county building to do some good old-fashioned manual research. Various types of licenses are examples of another type of public record. Let's say your subject claims to be a barber. Well, all barbers have to be licensed. Where do you think that list exists? Right. Public records. How about court records? Do you think that they could be beneficial?

Social networks. It never ceases to amaze me to discover what people have put out on the open Internet for the world to see via either a photo or a statement. This may provide you with an inside line into how the subject actually thinks or who or what he might be involved with. So, your subject looks great on paper, impeccable resume, good references, and stellar background, but when you look on Facebook, you happen to find a recent picture posted of your subject smoking a joint and wearing the colors of an organized outlaw motorcycle gang. What does that do to your risk rating?

FinCEN 314b.[4] This is only for authorized financial institutions. The USA PATRIOT Act enabled financial institutions to share information with each other. If bank A is looking for some information on a subject, it can submit a request to FinCEN. FinCEN, after reviewing the request, will send out an e-mail blast to all the appropriate financial institutions. Every financial institution should have a designated 314 person whose function is to review all the incoming FinCEN 314b requests and determine whether the subject is one of its customers. If the subject is a customer, then FinCEN would advise bank A, and a direct request via FinCEN could be made to that financial institution. Also, your institution may have a list of all the FinCEN 314 contacts at various banks, and you can send them a prefabricated form directly.

Specialized vendor databases. There are many of types of tools on the market. Each is different in its size and scope. Many are custom designed specifically for your institution, some are off the shelf, and some have completely customizable parameters. Some databases are built specifically to be used as an all-in-one AML tool, and some are single purpose. For example, one vendor database may be used just for OFAC. Another might be for determining politically exposed persons. Other databases may incorporate transaction monitoring and alert generations. Some are for case support and reporting. Many provide analytics, create graphs, and perform visual analysis. There are many vendors selling software. Having the appropriate software from a vendor that fits your needs is a great way to streamline your process, memorialize your findings, and maintain quality records.[5]

For government personnel, the issues do not change regarding the Internet and the invisible Web. However, many of the other "pay" databases may not be at your immediate disposal unless the money comes out of your own pocket. The agency you are employed with may affect your access to various records. A small local police department, for example, will not usually have direct access to many of the financial databases (such as the FinCEN database). Even large federal agencies don't usually have access to another agency's database (much like banks don't have access to each other's proprietary databases). If you are in a special task force setting (like I was with the New York HIFCA El Dorado Task Force), then you probably have the best of all worlds because each task force member brings with him his agency's database. Fortunately, the advent of the Regional Intelligence Centers (such as the NY HIDTA) can now provide most all law enforcement with access to multiple databases. The sources of intelligence become much greater as more information becomes available to you. Further, once some type of reason for inquiry has been established, the power of the subpoena kicks in, and that opens up quite a few more doors.

FinCEN has a program specifically for law enforcement access. It is called FinCEN Gateway. It is not available to everyone, and it has certain criteria that must be met and subsequently followed. Usually one person from an agency or regional intelligence center will be granted access. The portal allows you to review the various reporting forms that have been submitted to FinCEN, such as SARs and currency transaction reports (CTRs).

Other Special Considerations

Some of the following topics have been mentioned previously in Chapter 4, However, since much of the AML process with these components has to do with KYC/CIP, I will go over them in a little more detail.

Transaction Monitoring

Transaction monitoring is pretty much exactly what it sounds like. Each and every transaction that a customer makes is reviewed. This is done through the use of specific transaction-monitoring software. Each financial institution, according to size, customer base, products offered, and budget will have a unique set of parameters for their software. The purpose of the software is to identify any potential unusual transactions, patterns, and activity. For example, say a small Ma and Pa pizza shop that historically generates approximately $20,000 a month in sales suddenly starts making large cash deposits totaling approximately $100,000 for the month. There could be a legitimate reason, of course. However, because of the rare and unusual nature of the transactions, this incident should be flagged by the transaction-monitoring software and marked for further review and analysis by the AML team to attempt to determine whether the transactions rise to the level of suspicious.

Therein lies the second phase of transaction monitoring: the enhanced due diligence phase. Because of a certain trigger event (alert) that was generated by the transaction monitoring software, the event must now be reviewed and either cleared or escalated for additional review (further review could mean a SAR or even exiting the relationship with the customer).

All results must be notated and documented. If the event is cleared, why was it cleared? Based upon what additional information? If the event is to be escalated, it should be noted, and then the next-level reviewer is responsible for memorializing their findings. For every action there is a re-action; notate it.

One of the biggest issues with a transaction-monitoring program is the ability to set the software so that it does not miss any unusual activity but does not generate too many false positives. It is a bit of a balancing act at first, but eventually an appropriate medium is found. This system should be reviewed frequently to determine whether it is capturing and identifying unusual activity as designed. Additionally, the system should be monitored for the purpose of statistics and assessing any trends and patterns.

Correspondent Banking - Know Your Correspondents

I'll quickly review correspondent accounts. A small bank in a foreign country may have customers who need access to the U.S. financial system. Perhaps they have clients in the United States or need to purchase goods in the United States. Unfortunately, the small foreign bank has no offices in the United States, and therefore its customers will find it difficult to conduct business relations without access to a U.S. bank. Hence, the concept of the *correspondent bank* was created. The small foreign bank enters into a corresponding relationship with a U.S. bank. This relationship allows the small foreign bank's customers to make and receive payments in the United States. This type of relationship is common for many types of international trade, particularly if payments must be made in currency (in other words, dollars, yen, rupees, and so on) that is not their own.

Correspondent banking has its own unique set of risk factors. In your typical correspondent relationship, financial institutions are faced with the nearly impossible task of having to know their customer's customer. Really? Yes. It is quite impossible to be 100 percent sure of someone's identity unless you actually did the due diligence on the subject for the corresponding bank. Of course, that is not going to happen. The due diligence is going to be done, or ideally be done, by the other bank, known as the respondent bank. You can only hope that they do as they say they will and perform the due diligence to an acceptable degree.

That leaves only one reasonable choice for a domestic financial institution, and that is to make sure you have done due diligence on the corresponding bank itself during the onboarding application period. That particular due diligence includes the following:

- Knowing the corresponding bank's management

    a.   Where the corresponding bank is incorporated and domiciled

    b.   Publicly traded or privately owned

c.

Structure of the corresponding bank's management

d.   Whether there are PEPs in the executive management

- Being aware of the country risk
- Obtaining a copy of the corresponding bank's policies and procedures (specifically, obtaining the policy on how the corresponding bank conducts KYC on its customers)

To help you through this process is a document referred to as the Wolfsberg Questionnaire.[6] This is a short form to assist institutions with due diligence on a corresponding bank.

After you have reviewed all the policies of the corresponding bank and you feel comfortable that your corresponding partner will do their job appropriately, then you may proceed. If in the end it turns out that the corresponding bank did not do their job as they advertised, at least your regulating examiner will be able to determine that you did everything that you possibly could in this circumstance to maintain a quality CIP program.

Politically Exposed Persons

The Financial Action Task Force (FATF) defines politically exposed persons (PEPS) as follows: "individuals who are or have been entrusted with prominent public functions in a foreign country, for example Heads of State, or government officials, senior politicians, judicial or military officials, senior executives of state owned corporations, important political party officials."[7] Business relationships with family members or close associates of PEPs involved in reputational risks similar to those with PEPs themselves."

In other words, a PEP can be a senior political figure, a member of his immediate family, or a close associate. Keep in mind, once a PEP, always a PEP (99.9% true – there is always an exception to a rule) The risk posed by these individuals is that their funds may be the proceeds of foreign corruption and that those illegally obtained funds are laundered through the bank.

Deciphering whether a person is a PEP is usually handled by the same or similar third-party vendor that scrubs all the transactions for any OFAC sanctions. Any final decision as to the risk mitigation of a PEP is usually handled by bank management after reviewing the customer, his position, his source of funds, his geography, and a number of other risk factors. PEPS can be both foreign and domestic.

Note
Deciding the risk posed by a PEP is usually handled by the financial institution's top management. If in doubt, kick it upstairs (escalate).

KYC potential red flags There is certainly no shortage of potential red flags for KYC/CIP. Here are some of the most common red flags. It should be noted that just because a trigger event occurs or a red flag is observed does not mean that the customer is a bad guy. In fact, most red flags turn out to have a legitimate circumstance. But, it is those few and far between incidents that may spell trouble. However, the financial institution must examine each trigger like it is the real deal. Assume the worst and hope for the best.

- *The subject presents incomplete, conflicting, or incorrect details.*
- *The subject is hesitant or unwilling to provide details of business activities.*
- *The subject does not provide a phone number.*
- *The subject provides only a post-office box for an address.*

The same address is used by several other subjects.

- Accounts have been opened or attempted to be opened using a variation of the same name or something similar.
- Be alert to copies of documents presented to you by the subject.
- The subject reports income far greater than the standard norm for someone in the same field.
- The transaction pattern is inconsistent with the account-opening statements.

Summary

Now you know that a quality KYC/CIP program is the heart of the AML process. The CIP process begins at the onset of customer–financial institution relationship and never ends until the account is closed. Computerized software plays a prominent role in reviewing all transactions and filtering out unusual scenarios. Due diligence is the crux of the program. Appropriate and through due diligence is done via proper investigative techniques.

Each of the aforementioned categories discussed are themselves topics for books, articles, and seminars. The funny thing about this industry is that as soon as you think you know the topic, something new pops up that you have to wrap your head around. Here are some words of advice: Never stop reading. Things change quickly, and a financial institution or government official should be keenly aware of events and dynamics.

Next up is one of my favorite topics, the suspicious activity report. This book will point out what it is, why it is done, how to properly prepare a SAR, and what happens to the SAR once it leaves the financial institution.

Footnotes

1 Sullivan, Kevin. "The Investigative Mind," *ACAMS Today*. April 2010.

2 *Compstat*: Computer statistics. A management tool used by law enforcement similar to Six Sigma and Total Quality Management theories.

3 *I highly recommend a person I have known for years and to this day amazes me with something new every time I take a class or read an article by her. Her name is Cynthia Hetherington, and she can be located at* https://www.hetheringtongroup.com/training.shtml .

4 *FinCEN: The Financial Crimes Enforcement Network. A U.S. Department of the Treasury agency whose mission is to safeguard the financial system from illicit use and combat money laundering. 314b is the section of the USA PATRIOT Act that allows sharing of information between financial institutions under certain circumstances.*

5 I hesitate to mention software companies by name as to keep myself totally impartial. Just do an Internet search for *AML software*.

6 You can find the Wolsfberg Questionnaire at www.wolfsberg-principles.com/pdf/home/Wolfsberg-Anti-Money-Laundering-Questionnaire-2014.pdf .

7 www.fatf-gafi.org/media/fatf/documents/recommendations/guidance-pep-rec12-22.pdf.

6. A SAR Is Born

(1)

While I was in the money-laundering task force in Manhattan, we made it our mission to read every Bank Secrecy Act–related suspicious activity report (SAR) that was submitted by every financial institution in New York. We would routinely read approximately 4,000 SARs each month. Additionally, we developed and conducted regular SAR review meetings that had multiple federal, state, and local law enforcement and regulatory agencies in attendance.

Because of my position, I had the unique capacity to read, examine, and analyze SARs from every financial institution. It was interesting to see how the SARs transformed from pre-9/11 to post-9/11. In the early days after 9/11, many financial institutions were still reluctant to file, and if they did, the prevailing theory was to keep the information in the narrative to a minimum. During those days, many legal compliance departments, which had the last word on the SARs, felt that sharing too much of the bank's information might be viewed as some type of privacy violation or abuse of customer trust or was just a plain old fear of the unknown.

That era was followed by the defensive filing era. This was an era born of frustration by the banks, which were getting scolded by the regulators for not filing SARs. So, they turned to filing SARs on just about everything, although some institutions still held to the "don't put much information in the narrative" mantra.

At about this point (probably around 2003 or 2004), there was much confusion. Bankers were complaining that different regulating bodies were telling them different things, and even various examiners within the same regulatory bodies were providing conflicting guidance. This was compounded by law enforcement complaining that they were not receiving the proper information on the SARs. Law enforcement was pointing the finger at the financial institutions, which in turn were pointing the finger at the regulators for providing guidance that was apparently not consistent with what law enforcement was looking for. It was a bit of a mess, with most entities trying to do the right thing. Yet there was just too much confusion as to how this process should play out.

Finally, in 2005, the Federal Financial Institutions Examination Council (FFIEC), a formal interagency body created to prescribe uniform principles and standards in the supervision of financial institutions, developed the FFIEC manual[1] in conjunction with various regulatory bodies and law enforcement. It took into consideration many of the raw complaints from financial institutions. This was a guidebook for all examiners that provided them with a uniform and systematic review procedure. The result was that much of the confusion was eliminated. It was a godsend at the time, and it did wonders to put everyone at least in the same ballpark. While there may never be total three-part harmony between financial institutions, regulators, and law enforcement, it sure did get a lot closer and provided a reference point for everyone. Subsequently, the FFIEC has updated the manual to address more concerns and to add sections on some new methods of potential money laundering. I imagine that the manual will be a staple in the fight against money laundering for a long time to come.

The Back Story

The SAR (referred to as a *suspicious transaction report* in many countries outside of the United States) is the bane of the anti-money laundering (AML) process. The SAR is the handshake between the financial institutions and law enforcement, considering that much of the financial institution's AML efforts are performed with the intention of providing law enforcement with a heads-up if suspicious behavior is afoot. Writing a complete and through SAR becomes one of the most important functions that a financial institution can perform.

I'll break down this chapter for both the financial institution folk and the law enforcement sector because both have separate responsibilities with regard to the SAR. For the financial institution crowd, I will discuss how to identify "suspicious," what the narrative should consist of, and what happens after the SAR is completed. Law enforcement members will become familiar with the financial institution process, what is and is not available to you with and without the requirement of a subpoena, and how the financial reverse engineering process works.

Note

The era of SARs in the United States began with the Annunzio-Wylie Anti-Money Laundering Act of 1992, which required regulated financial institutions to report transactions that they suspected might involve illicit funds or purposes. The USA PATRIOT Act of 2001 upped the ante to include securities broker and dealers. Then in 2006, the Bank Secrecy Act (BSA) was amended to require insurance companies to begin filing SARs. Other industries have a voluntary SAR reporting status.

Getting to Suspicious

One of the most frequent questions that I get—and that FinCEN gets—is, "When should I file a SAR?" The term *suspicious*, in and of itself, is a bit nebulous. There is no absolute answer for this question. The fact is that "suspicious" depends on many factors. What is suspicious for one institution may not be for another. Much depends on the risk assessment performed on the client, considering financial history, geography, products, other entities involved, frequency, and economic sense of the transaction and incident. Further, individual knowledge and experience play a role. Hence, the more informed, the more experienced, the more knowledgeable on the topic of money laundering a person is, then the wider but stronger the net that is cast becomes.

In many cases, an incident, trigger or "alert" will be generated by the financial institution's computerized transaction-monitoring system. Parameters will have been set by the third-party vendor that sold and maintains the system, in conjunction with the individual financial institution's specific requirements. Obviously, parameters are set differently depending upon the type of financial institution you are, based on the size, demographics, geography, and products offered. However, sometimes an incident does not even get "scrubbed" through the system because the particular incident might not even have been a transaction (it could have been an attempted transaction or simply an application for an account).

For example, perhaps the incident was someone trying to establish an account and, upon gathering the potential customer's CIP, a giant red flag popped up that sent the hair on the back of your neck into a tizzy. Usually, an incident or alert would start out being considered as unusual. In fact, "unusual" is the preferred term because at this point you should not classify it as suspicious because of considerations of time restraints that I will cover shortly. Once an incident makes your "spidey senses" tingle, then it should be escalated so that enhanced due diligence is performed on the customers or other entities. Refer to Chapter 5 for more about due diligence in the CIP.

The following is per the Bank Secrecy Act (31 CFR 103.18)[2]: *For any known or suspected violation of federal criminal laws or regulations committed/attempted against or through the institution if it involves or aggregates at least $5,000 in funds or other assets and the bank knows, suspects, or has reason to suspect the funds are:*

- *Obtained from illegal activity*
- *Intended or conducted to hide or disguise funds or assets derived from illegal activity*

Designed to evade any reporting requirements of the Bank Secrecy Act What the BSA is saying is that there is a $5,000 floor for filing a SAR. In other words, if the suspicious activity constitutes less than a $5,000 transaction or even perhaps no transaction at all, then it is not required to be reported. Personally, I think anything you deem to be suspicious should be filed no matter what the economic amount involved is. In fact, as per the FATF 40 Recommendations, there is no floor limit on an STR (FATF calls it a suspicious transaction report). While the amount may fall well below the $5,000 threshold at your institution, you never know if the same client is doing similar activities at other institutions. Hence, I believe you should file no matter the amount. It certainly can't hurt. However, I understand the reluctance of an institution to file when it then becomes mandated to review the incident again in 90 days, especially if manpower is short (and what institution is not short on employees?).

Hidden Value of SARs

Even if an incident does not appear to the financial institution to be useful to law enforcement, I caution you to make sure that you do what you are required to do and allow law enforcement to worry about a SAR's usefulness. There are some reasons why something that looks like a dud to the financial institution could be a gem to law enforcement.

Perhaps law enforcement is investigating the subject based upon a SAR from another institution that you aren't aware of. While your SAR might not have originally been a top selection for further investigation, it might help indicate a pattern or furnish additional information about the subject. Remember, you see only the SARs that you create. There may be numerous other SARs on your customer/subject or of the same type of incident that have been filed by several other financial institutions. Various trends and patterns might be observed based on the type of activity, geography, name, business, address, phone number, or other identifier depicted in the narrative section that could relate to another SAR or investigation that law enforcement is handling.

30/60/90 Rule

I mentioned time restraints earlier. Let me elaborate. You have 30 days to file a SAR with FinCEN once you have determined an incident to be suspicious. Hence, this is why you use the word *unusual* initially. Until you perform you due diligence or enhanced due diligence, then the incident is unusual. Once the investigation reveals other information or is unable to make sense of the incident, then it should be labeled as *suspicious*, and a SAR should be completed and filed.

The filing time frame may be extended to 60 days if the identity of the subject cannot be established.

Once a SAR has been filed, you now are provided 90 days before you need to review the matter. As such time, upon review, it will be determined that there have been no further incidents or alerts, the activity is continuing, or the account has been exited. If the activity is continuing, you can choose to complete another SAR or perhaps your preference is to exit the relationship. Whatever you do, be sure to document your actions and be able to justify them. The regulators when performing an audit will be sampling your SARs, and you need to have everything in order.

While I am talking about time frames, the financial institution must maintain a copy of that SAR and any supporting documentation used to make that suspicious determination for a period of no less than five years.

Completing the SAR

Once the financial institution has completed its investigation, the results should be reviewed by senior management or the legal staff before they are sent to FinCEN. The SAR is now a completely online document[3] that, once completed, is directly transmitted to FinCEN. The new online format has made things a bit easier for both the filers and the reviewers. Every box has a corresponding drop-down list. There should be no empty boxes on a SAR that you think is ready to go. The more difficult part is the narrative section. This area, which allows for approximately 17,000 characters, is the place where you get to tell your story. This is also the section that seems to give many people trouble. The usual question is, "What do I put in here?" I have seen everything from great to horrible in this area. I have seen too much information, too little information, information that appears to be written in Greek, information that pertains to nothing, and information that contains too many acronyms that I had never seen before and apparently are institution specific. My favorite SAR of all time was one that the entire narrative read, "We are filing a SAR because we feel the customer's activity is suspicious." That was the whole thing. Perhaps not the most insightful SAR of all time.

A fundamentally good SAR narrative should contain the following:

- The basic Ws and H: who, what, when, where, why (although the why might not be clear), and how

    - Who is conducting the suspicious activity? And, are there any other subjects or entities involved? Provide as much pedigree information that you have on the subject (a quality KYC program should provide all the pertinent information on identification). Obtain all addresses, phone numbers, and e-mail address. Don't forget to mention if there are any other signers on the account. My pet peeve is something like "Occupation: Consultant or Importer/Exporter." Please provide additional information such as what the person is a consultant on and whom he works for.

    - What is the activity that is suspicious? What instruments were used? Wire transfers, ATMs, shell companies, or foreign currency? Identify the source of funds.

    - When was the activity detected? When did the suspicious activity occur? Over what period of time? Any previous filings?

    - Where did the activity occur? Identify all the locations impacted by this activity. Identify all accounts involved.

    - Why is the activity suspicious? Is it unusual for the customer, product type, or services offered by the institution? Is there any legitimate business purpose for the transaction?

    - How did the suspicious activity occur? Was it a one-time event? A series of transactions? What was the source of funds? Track the flow of the funds from beginning to end.

- Do not use acronyms. Each financial institution has its own vernacular and jargon that may be used only by that institution. I can't tell you how many times I read a SAR and had no idea of what the writer was talking about. Don't use in-house acronyms. Write it so your mother could understand it.

- If the basis of the SAR is money coming in, elaborate on how it goes out. The same goes for outgoing funds: Tell how they got into the account in the first place.
- Try to write the body in chronological order.
- Include spreadsheets when necessary; with the new on-line SAR forms, spreadsheets can now be added to the SAR as attachments.
- If you are listing numerous transactions, dates, locations, and other numbers, I suggest you summarize. Nothing will cause the reviewer's eyes to glaze over faster than pages of numbers. If law enforcement would like further specifics on the dates and times, they will contact you.

  - For example: Mr. X made 27 deposits, each under $10,000, on separate days between April 1 and May 15, 2014.

- Be short but informative. No need to rewrite *War and Peace*. Conversely, one or two sentences are not quite enough. Write to inform, not to impress.
- FinCEN has published a detailed report on constructing a SAR, available on the agency's web site.[4]

The narrative should be organized in three layers. There should be a clear introduction that details who the financial institution is and a brief synopsis (just a few sentences) and general description of the suspicious activity. Note any previous SARs completed and any internal case numbers. This should be followed by the body of the narrative. The body should contain all the facts and statistics that are pertinent to the report. List all the dates and accounts involved and detail the transactions. Finally, there should be a conclusion. Summarize all your findings and any follow-up action that may have been conducted by the institution, particularly if the relationship has been exited.

There are some common mistakes that should be recognized.

- Incomplete or inaccurate information

  - All boxes should be populated. If proper KYC was done, then much of the pedigree information should be readily available.

  - Not listing the total dollar amount

  - If this is not the first SAR written on this subject/entity, then notate how many other SARs have been submitted and notate the total amount considered suspicious to date in addition to the amount of this particular SAR.

- Not listing the date range of the activity

- It is important for investigators to know whether this activity is occurring over a one-month time frame or whether this activity has been ongoing for a much longer time.

- Not noting the money in and money out.
- Most importantly, detail whether law enforcement has been contacted and include the name, agency, and number of the law enforcement contact if possible.
- Not notating other subjects or information.

  - When law enforcement reviews the SAR, they will run checks on the names you provide. Many times those names will not generate any triggers. However, oftentimes, an associate of the subject or an address may pop up as a red flag. Therefore, in the narrative, notate any other information about associates of the subject.

Here is additional SAR completion information:

- Don't leave any blank boxes. If the answer is unknown, then say so in the drop-down menu. You will get an error message if all the critical fields are not completed.

- In the pre-online days, attachments were not allowed. Now they are accepted. However, this is not a replacement for the narrative.

- Put the reason to close the account.

  - The risk level is too high.
  - The customer refused to provide information.
  - You have firsthand knowledge of illegal activity.

- What may seem insignificant to you may be the missing piece of the puzzle for law enforcement.

- Law enforcement may not adopt a case the first time they review a SAR. It may take a couple of SARs before law enforcement determines that the situation should be investigated.

In general, the narrative section of the SAR historically seems to be the area of most trepidation, mostly because of years of confusing and conflicting information being floated by a variety of sources. Let me give you the "in a nutshell" answer. The SAR narrative should not be a literary gem. Law enforcement is not Oprah's book club. Law enforcement does not want long and drawn-out narratives. They are looking for the financial institution to cut to the chase. They don't care about the legal disclaimers; they just want the facts. Make it short and sweet. Tell law enforcement why it is that the financial institution feels that this incident is suspicious. In other words, why is the hair on the back of your neck standing up? Provide them with the facts that surround that feeling. What did the financial institution do to investigate? Do not use jargon or acronyms that are specific to the institution. Law enforcement has no clue when the financial institution mentions their own forms (for example, form XYZ123 may be a form in only one particular bank, not in all banks). The same goes for various accounts (for example, a preferred account). Use language that everyone can relate to. Finally, write the narrative as if you were writing a letter to your mother and telling her what was going on. Would Mom understand what you are saying?

Obviously not all reported SARs become law enforcement cases nor do all SARs become investigations. Everyone understands that there are those SARs filed strictly for defensive purposes. Further, most SARs are not going to turn into a major investigation by law enforcement. Don't be upset when the SARs that your financial institution completes never generate any law enforcement activity. The bottom line is that you never know if other financial institutions have done similar SARs on the same subject and an investigation is proceeding. Also, be aware that many times the AML analyst or investigator at a financial institution may never even be informed by the institution that a subpoena has be submitted (depending upon the size of the institution).

Why Financial Institutions Need to File

There have been many incidents in the last few years where SARs, or lack thereof, have been the crux of regulatory fines for numerous institutions. Financial institutions have been hammered for failing to file SARs, failing to file SARs in a timely manner, failing to have complete and thorough SARs, and failing to train AML personnel properly. Further, a poorly written SAR can sap manpower time and effort when it has to be rewritten and reviewed. If this happens frequently, regulators may have a jaded view of your institution's ability to maintain a quality AML program. Hence, precious resources are expended to rectify the issue.

Why bother doing a SAR if you have to return to it in 90 days? Well, if you don't complete a SAR when one is obviously required, your regulator will hammer you during their audit. The funny thing is that if you don't complete a SAR, you still have to describe your investigative finding and detail why you decided not to write the SAR. Basically, you have to write almost as much telling why you did not compete a SAR than if you had just done the darn SAR. You might as well do it correctly right from the get-go. No financial institution wants to be fined by the regulators, and certainly they don't want to damage their reputation in the eyes of the public or shareholders.

What Happens After You File

All SARs are forwarded to FinCEN, which will categorize and review the SARs. FinCEN will create statistics based upon the information provided in the various drop-down boxes on the SAR online form. Those results are detailed and published in FinCEN's SAR Activity Review and are available to anyone via FinCEN's web site.

For the law enforcement folks, FinCEN makes the SARs available to certain federal, state, and local law enforcement agencies. Just as the confidentiality of the SAR is mandated at the financial institution level, so it is at the law enforcement level. There, officials are allowed to discuss the SARs with each other only under certain circumstances, such as for the purposes of investigating money laundering, terrorist financing, or other crimes. Once a SAR is in law enforcement's hands, it is considered a confidential document and is not to be disclosed to the subject listed on the SAR or to another financial institution.

In various geographical areas, law enforcement agencies gather together to discuss SARs that relate to their particular concerns. This is normally referred to as a SAR review meeting. (There are SAR review teams in numerous location all throughout the country.) Such meetings are held periodically and are usually attended by representatives of law enforcement agencies at the federal, state, and local levels and by federal and state prosecutors and regulators.

Many cases have been developed as a direct result of these SAR review meetings. I have often referred to this as *case reverse engineering*. Normally, law enforcement makes an arrest of a subject for a crime and then tries to figure out where the money is that is attached to that crime. However, when obtaining intelligence as a result of a SAR, law enforcement is advised of the amount and location of the money and now has to try to figure out the crime that goes hand in hand with that cash.

Law Enforcement Contact

Once law enforcement decides that a particular SAR is of interest to them, they will begin their due diligence. Eventually, law enforcement may need to contact the financial institution. Contact with the financial institution will usually come via a subpoena.[5] The subpoena will usually be forwarded to the financial institution's legal compliance department. At this time, the financial institution should have a system to memorialize the pertinent information such as the date the subpoena was received, the name of the agent and agency, the customer's name or account number, and the date the request was fulfilled.

Other methods of law enforcement contact is via a search warrant or a freeze order. The same rules apply to financial institutions; they should memorialize the request, respond in a timely fashion, and never ever ignore a legal governmental request.

The usual turnaround time from the date of a request to the date the information is sent to the requesting agent is usually somewhere between two to six weeks depending upon the size and scope of the financial institution and the requested information. It is not a bad idea to have someone in the legal department at the financial institution call the requesting agent and ask whether they require all the requested information ASAP or can some information be kept at the ready. Many times (particularly at the beginning of an investigation) the agent is simply looking for the basics (for example, account statements, checks, credit cards). While the subpoena may look like a laundry list, sometimes law enforcement wants just the basics; however, if they need more information, the financial institution already has a subpoena on file. Contacting the agent can save everyone time.

Another way for information to be passed along legally is called the *supporting documentation rule*, which is title 31 of the Code of Federal Regulations (31CFR103.18 Availability of Information). This allows law enforcement to obtain detailed information from financial institutions without the requirement of a subpoena. The detailed information consists of the various supporting documents that the financial institution referenced when it performed due diligence prior to creating the SAR. Many times, law enforcement agencies that are reviewing SARs found one SAR that appears to have potential yet have not decided to open a full investigation just yet, so they may send a request to the financial institution for supporting documentation. Then upon those results. law enforcement may open a full-scale investigation, and more than likely a subpoena will follow.

The actual SAR supporting documentation rule is as follows:

Institutions filing SARs are directed to maintain all "supporting documentation" related to the activity being reported. Disclosure of supporting documentation related to the activity that is being reported on a SAR does not require a subpoena, court order or other judicial or *administrative process. Under the SAR regulations, financial institutions are <u>required to disclose</u> supporting documentation to appropriate law enforcement agencies, or FinCEN, upon request.*

Suspicious Activity Report Statistics

One of the responsibilities of FinCEN is to compile statistics from all the SARs submitted. The stats are broken down by industry type such as depository institutions (banks and credit unions), money service businesses, casino and card clubs, insurance companies, securities and futures, and other financial institutions. The data that FinCEN collects is extremely valuable to financial institutions, regulators, and law enforcement. It lets the U.S. Treasury Department review events deemed to be suspicious by financial institutions and react in any number of ways. The response by the government is metered by the degree and frequency of the activity reported. When all three players (financial institutions, regulators, and law enforcement) work together, then SARs become a tremendous asset in fighting money laundering and terrorist financing. The theory is that if the government can hinder money-laundering activities, then the predicate crime (the illegal activity that generated the ill-gotten gains) associated with the funds will be curtailed.

The Figure 6-1 and Table 6-1 indicate the amount of SARS that have been reported in 2013 and 2014

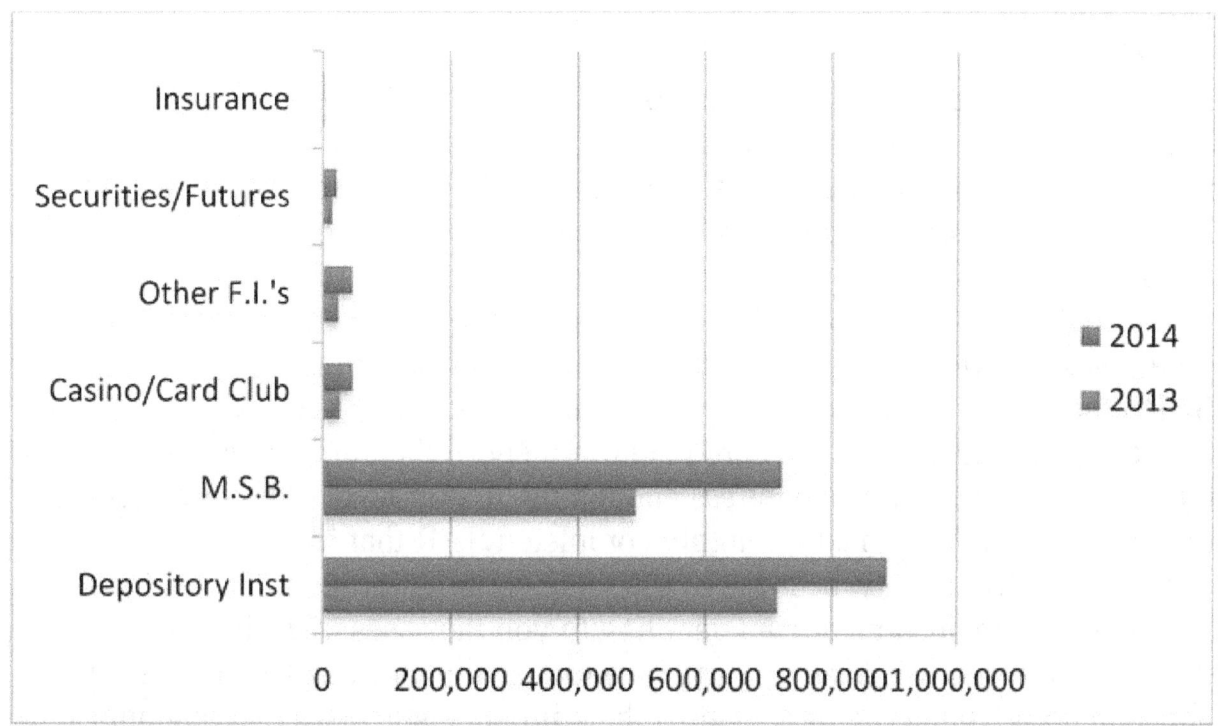

Figure 6-1. Number of SARS reported

Table 6-1. 2013/2014 SAR Stats

Depository institutions	714,000
Money service businesses	491,000
Casinos/card clubs	27,500
Other financial institutions	25,000
Securities/futures	15,500
Insurance	3,000

   By far the greatest number of SARs are written and reported for potential structuring activity. However, there is a multitude of other reasons that SARs are written, such as fraud, various potential BSA violations, and counterfeiting, just to name a few. One of the reasons why it is required to complete the drop-down boxes on the SAR reporting form is for the purpose of statistical analysis and recognizing various trends and patterns. You can find this information in one of two publications created by FinCEN: "SARS by the Numbers"[6] and "SAR Activity Review – Trends, Tips & Issues."[7] Both of these publications should be required reading for anyone involved in the AML business. My further suggestion is for all AML personnel to bookmark the FinCEN.gov web site because it contains a wealth of information.

Summary

Remember, SARs are confidential. Do not share any information about the subject of a SAR with anyone outside of your immediate unit, supervisor, legal department, or appropriate law enforcement, and certainly do not share any information with the person or entity involved in the transaction that prompted the SAR.

A myth that I often hear is that the SARs go into some governmental black hole and are never seen again. Nothing could be further from the truth. The SARS that financial institutions complete are read—maybe not every single one in every jurisdiction, but many are read routinely, and others are read as required by law enforcement. I cannot stress enough the importance of the information that is provided through a thoroughly completed SAR that includes a quality narrative. Unfortunately, because of the same confidentially rule I mentioned previously, I am prevented from detailing to you the cases that I investigated as a direct result of a SAR. You will just have to take my word that SARs are an absolute home run in the fight against the criminal enterprises that attempt to make use of money laundering.

Some law enforcement agencies have been reviewing SARs for years, while others are new to the game. Many are just beginning to realize the wonderful investigative tool that SARS and other financial reports can be. Financial institutions, regulators, and law enforcement all have a similar goal, and that is to keep the bad guys from abusing the financial system. Cooperation, understanding, and solidarity among all can give you an edge on the bad guys.

Footnotes

1 You can find the FFIEC manual at
   https://www.ffiec.gov/bsa_aml_infobase/pages_manual/manual_online.htm.

2 U.S. Code of Federal Regulations Title 31 section 103.18.

3 http://bsaefiling.fincen.treas.gov/main.html.

4 FinCEN publishes the "SAR Activity Report" bi-annually and a "SARs by the Numbers" report at least annually and sometimes more frequently than that. You can find the web site at the following URLs:

5 *Subpoena*: A government agency request for the production of documents or to appear in court.

6 www.fincen.gov/news_room/rp/sar_by_number.html.

7 www.fincen.gov/news_room/rp/sar_tti.html.

7. Tips for Law Enforcement and Financial Crimes Investigators

☒

(1)

In today's law enforcement environment, the mission remains the same as it always was: to protect and serve. State, city, and local police are spread thin, and any violent crime will always get attention, manpower, and any available funding. I'm not saying that is wrong (it is not); I'm just stating a fact. Putting together a financial crimes unit is not usually high on the priority list of the ivory tower or the powers that be—or, it wasn't until someone mentioned the term *asset seizure*. Done appropriately, a financial crimes unit (FCU) just might pay for itself and then some. If having a full-fledged FCU is not possible, then perhaps someone could be assigned to a multi-agency task force where any assets seized are split among the participating law enforcement agencies. I was part of a federal task force that operated in this manner. Usually, when the case is over and all the paperwork is completed, the seizure amount is divided among agencies according to the number of personnel and manpower hours that went into the investigation, so the more personnel, the bigger piece of the seizure pie. In many cases there is one person from each agency assigned to seizures, and it's that person's job to be on top of all the paperwork and administrative procedures.

Why bother? Well, how about a few facts for some clarity? According to the FBI, the amount of money taken during all bank robberies in 2011 was more than $38 million. The amount of money thought be laundered yearly is in the neighborhood of $2 *trillion*. Where do you think all that money laundering funds comes from? One of the reasons to attempt to put the kibosh on money laundering is to prevent bad guys from reaping the proceeds of their crimes and funding additional crimes or acts of terror. Profit, remember, is an essential aspect of most crimes. Ironically, law enforcement puts tremendous effort when there is a report of a bank robbery, with manpower, helicopters, and K9s (and don't get me wrong, this is as they should). However, financial crimes such as check fraud, credit card fraud, and money laundering don't always receive the same treatment. Further, over the years on many occasions, I have seen perpetrators of financial crimes receive barely a slap on the wrist while a more traditional criminal gets a much longer sentence. It's a bit of a disparity, but I do think that gap is closing as financial crimes get more media attention. Having a strong antimoney laundering unit is therefore worth the effort. You are trying to take down organized criminal enterprises and terrorists moving tons of money, not just a couple of mules or runners moving small amounts. For example, would you rather focus on someone selling loose joints or the kingpin of the drug cartel? Putting away mules is great, but that is just a means to an end and not the end itself. The same theory applies to money laundering. Arresting the two mules making an exchange in the parking lot of the mall is nice; however, the case should not end there. Law enforcement should have a system in place to escalate the investigation.

This chapter is dedicated to both the law enforcement investigator and the financial institution investigation team. Both of those entities should have an understanding of not just money laundering but of what information is available and how to proceed with sharing that information. Each side, law enforcement and the financial institution, may have different end goals (law enforcement to arrest and convict and gain more intelligence and financial institutions to detect, deter, and protect the institution).

The "You Must Be An Accountant Theory"

Many times members of the law enforcement community will ask me, "You have to be an accountant to be in the money laundering unit, don't you?" I respond with, "You don't have to be chemist to work as a narcotics investigator, do you? You don't have to be a pathologist to work as a homicide investigator, do you? Well, guess what? You don't have to be an accountant to work as a financial crimes investigator."

Chemists, pathologists, and accountants are, of course, all specific professions whose services may be required in the long process of a criminal investigation. For example, in every drug case, somewhere along the way, the drugs have to be analyzed by the lab (chemist), which then provides official certification of the type of drug and the weight. Consequently, the need for a chemist is important. However, the chemist did not conduct the fundamental investigation and was certainly not the case agent. That's why an individual does not need a medical degree or to be a CPA to conduct an investigation. The basics of the investigation are, for the most part, all the same no matter what the particular subject is. Subsequent to the basics, specific investigative techniques are required to hone in on the particular subject matter of the investigation. So, let me be perfectly clear on this. You do not need to be an accountant to be a financial crimes investigator. You do, however, need to learn specific financial investigative techniques.

> **Note**
> Later in this chapter I will spell out all the steps that I took to get to where I am. This is not meant to be a template for becoming a financial crimes investigator but as an informational source for those readers who may have no one to turn to for guidance or perspective.

Perhaps one of the other reasons why the "you have to be an accountant" theory still lingers is in part because of the legend of one of the most famous money launderers, Al Capone. In the end, it was the accountant who did ol' Al in on charges of tax evasion. Kudos to the accountants. However, the laws were a bit different in 1931. While Capone certainly managed to do a heck of a job moving his money, he was never charged with money laundering. The reason for that was that there were no money-laundering statutes on the books. It was not until 1970, with the introduction of the Bank Secrecy Act (BSA), that money laundering was even addressed by the government. It was not until the Money Laundering Control Act of 1986 that money laundering became a federal crime. Using today's standards, Capone would be investigated by a team of investigators, agents, and detectives, and during the process, an accountant might be used to conduct what is referred to as *forensic accounting*.

Today, a professional money launderer (also called a *money broker*) is a profession that stands alone by itself. They might be lawyers, accountants, financial services advisors, or just some experienced individuals who know the system inside and out. These are the type of criminals who are difficult to catch. That's right out of Criminal Investigation 101—the smarter the criminal, the harder to catch. This is exactly why law enforcement needs to have appropriate training. Furthermore, with new technology and various new methods of money laundering, the training of law enforcement must be continual and up to date. In summation, accountants are necessary to complete their specific role. However, investigators must be the glue that puts the case together.

What Do Bankers Do

All of the bankers who law enforcement will most likely deal with are from the compliance section of the bank. (Please note that while I say bankers, I am also referring to broker/dealers, insurance companies, and money service businesses.) The compliance section can consist of the financial intelligence unit (FIU), the various fraud sections, the multitude of AML sections, the Office of Financial Assets Control (OFAC) at the bank, and the legal division. Their missions are different from law enforcement's mission. In law enforcement, the purpose is to try to build a successful case so officers can arrest, prosecute, and perhaps seize assets. A banker's mission is simply to deter, detect, and protect. The financial institution does not particularly focus on the prosecution of the money launderer. One reason is that anything that might bring negative media attention upon the bank would not look good from a public relations standpoint. The financial institution would much rather not be in that position, so if it can get rid of the issue before it becomes an issue, the financial institution will do so. Don't get me wrong here. There is nothing wrong with the financial institution's position. I am simply pointing out the differences.

One of the best things that law enforcement investigators and financial institution investigators can do is network. If as an investigator you really want to know what the banker does or if as a bank investigator you want to know what law enforcement does, talk to each other. An effort should be made to communicate on a regular basis. Many geographical areas have various associations, groups, or meetings where bankers and law enforcement get together to chat. Knowing someone, looking them in the eye, and shaking hands are so much more powerful than a cold call. The benefits are well worth the effort on both sides.

What Regulators Do

What about the regulators? Just who are they, and what do they do? It is important to note that financial institutions are private companies trying to maximize profit. There is nothing wrong with that. Financial institutions drive the economy, and as such, people and businesses the world over are tied to them. To provide the public with the confidence that their money is safe from abuse, the government created regulators to supervise the various standards (regulations) that have been developed. These regulations have been, and will continue to be, living, breathing elements because they change as new technologies enter the fray and as new banking relationships develop globally.

Different financial institutions have different regulators. For example, a state bank may be regulated by a state regulating authority. A national bank may be regulated by the Office of the Controller of the Currency. A credit union may be regulated by the National Credit Union Administration. A broker/dealer may be regulated by the Securities and Exchange Commission. There are numerous regulators, and an institution may have more than one regulator.

In a nutshell, regulators provide guidance on rules and regulations, and they conduct audits (reviews) of the financial institutions they supervise. Usually, this is performed on a yearly basis. It is up to the regulating authority to sample the work of the institution and determine whether the financial institution is doing its job appropriately. Regulators have the authority to impose a fine on the financial institution or even pull its charter and put them out of business. Because of this, financial institutions take the regulators seriously. I don't want to go too deep into the job functions of the regulators because that is not the purpose of this book. I just wanted to provide you with some basic information.

In effect, law enforcement and regulators don't have a particularly symbiotic relationship, at least not for most cases. At my previous job with the El Dorado, New York, HIFCA task force, regulators were actually part of the task force. However, that is not the norm. While there are always exceptions to this, for the most part the regulators do their thing with the financial institutions, and law enforcement does its thing, and rarely do they intersect. In some circumstances, law enforcement and regulators interacted via the suspicious activity report (SAR) review meetings. The regulators have access to the same SARs that law enforcement does. The difference is that law enforcement is looking for criminal activity, while the regulators are mostly focused on making sure that the financial institution is following predetermined standards. Regulators are usually helpful in providing a banking prospective when law enforcement's lack of banking experience results in a question about a banking situation. FinCEN (also a form of regulator) provides certain law enforcement members with the means to review all the SARs. Furthermore, FinCEN compiles stats that indicate various trends and patterns and publishes informative white papers. Besides being helpful to law enforcement, FinCEN asks for law enforcement's opinion of how things are going and what can be done to improve the process. (The FFIEC manual was produced to help regulating auditors address bank issues that were concerning to law enforcement, and FinCEN did ultimately update the SAR form.) Similar to the meetings between law enforcement and financial institutions, there should be meetings between regulators and law enforcement (Sometimes this is completed as part of a SAR review meeting. A point to note is that while financial institutions, regulators, and law enforcement may have "round tables" at various seminars, sometimes a financial institution member may temper and monitor their conversation with law enforcement if their regulator is sitting next to them. Further, bankers cannot attend the SAR review meeting because the information on the SARs is confidential to the contributing financial institution, law enforcement, and regulators and not available for review to all financial institutions.)

Who Are the Regulators?

There are many regulators, and sometimes it is difficult to figure out exactly who is responsible for the various entities. The following are general guidelines:

- *The Federal Reserve Bank*: Responsible for supervising and regulating bank holding companies, foreign banks with U.S. operations, and state-chartered banks that are members of the Federal Reserve System.
- *The Office of the Comptroller of the Currency (OCC):* Charters, regulates, and supervises all national commercial banks and federal savings associations.
- *Federal Deposit Insurance Company (FDIC)*: Regulates state-chartered banks that are not members of the Federal Reserve System. Additionally, the FDIC sells insurance to depository institutions, insuring a customer's account up to $250,000.
- *State bank*: Falls under the domain of both the state banking department of that particular state and also federal regulation.
- *National Credit Union Administration*: Regulates all credit unions.
- *Securities Exchange Commission*: Regulates all corporations that sell securities to the public and all securities broker/dealers.
- *Commodities Futures Trading Commission (CFTC)*: Regulates derivative trading. Its main goal is to prevent excessive speculation and manipulation of commodity prices.
- *Financial Industry Regulatory Authority (FINRA)*: Safeguards investors from fraud and bad practices. It regulates every brokerage firm and broker in the United States.

Getting in Touch with Regulators

For national banks, federal savings banks, and loan or thrift, visit www.ffiec.gov/consumercenter/default.aspx .

For state-chartered banks, savings institutions, and insurance companies, visit www.csbs.org/about/what/Pages/directory.aspx#.

For credit unions, visit www.ncua.gov/ .

SAR Power

For years law enforcement relied on leads from confidential informants and intelligence gleamed from arrests and investigations. There is nothing wrong with that, and it still continues as it should. But now there is the suspicious activity report. As mentioned earlier in the book, the SAR is a mandatory form that financial institutions complete when someone determines activity by a customer is beyond unusual. For example, a bank customer who is a hot dog vendor and has had an account for the past five years and has never deposited more than $10,000 in a month suddenly begins to make $50,000 a month in cash deposits. After the bank investigates the matter and determines that they have no reasonable explanation for the sudden change of activity by the hot dog vendor, the bank would complete a SAR. The SAR would be forwarded to FinCEN and then become available to certain members of law enforcement.

Note

Not all law enforcement members have access to the FinCEN portal. A law enforcement agency would need to be approved by FinCEN; then a member (or members) of that agency would have to complete a mandatory BSA compliance training program every two years. It is important to understand that not every police officer gets access to the FinCEN portal (usually just the badges that are involved with a financial crimes unit). Only approved agencies and personnel will be provided access.

Usually these SARs are reviewed by law enforcement and the regulators at SAR review meetings. (Financial institutions are not allowed at these meetings because of the confidentiality rules of the SARs.) Any further information about the incident would have to be requested either by subpoena or via the SAR supporting documentation rule to the submitting financial institution. These SAR review meetings are held in various jurisdictions all over the country. The information contained in the SARs could be valuable intelligence to begin an investigation. In fact, the whole SAR process could be considered a form of reverse engineering. Normally, law enforcement makes an arrest and then tries to find the money that goes with the crime. With a SAR, you are being told where and how much the money is, and now you have to find the associated crime that goes with that money.

SARs provide an abundance of leads. There are more than a million SARs completed each year, though not all of them will ever rise to the level of a law enforcement investigation. However, just because one SAR does not raise to the level that gets law enforcement interested, you must remember that other institutions may have completed and submitted a SAR (or SARs) on the same entity or perhaps a similar event. There have been and will continue to be quite a number of SARs that will lead to significant cases. (FinCEN details several of these cases on its web site.) This process is a treasure trove of information that should be utilized by law enforcement. If you are a large law enforcement agency (particularly one that has some type of financial crimes unit), you are amiss if you are not taking part in the SAR review meetings. These meetings not only provide valuable information but cross borders. Events in one jurisdiction of the country are not easily shared with other areas. Sometimes numerous representatives from different law enforcement agencies (within a regional area) will network and discover similar possible criminal events. Remember, the bad guys don't care about jurisdictions, but the good guys need to share information with each other.

Here are a few examples of SAR content and how it might be helpful to law enforcement:

- The initial SAR might not seem like much of a crime, perhaps just a low amount of money being moved, let's say $25,000. That's certainly not in the big-boy realm of seven digits. However, upon reading the narrative of the SAR, there is another name mentioned, perhaps the person who deposited the money in the bank but not the account holder. Upon checking the depositor's name, you note that he has been arrested twice before for sale of narcotics and is a known member of an organized criminal enterprise. Do you think that might change your mind about looking deeper into this SAR, even though the SAR amount is only $25,000? You bet your life it does!

- The initial SAR activity indicates a suspicious incident at a casino in Atlantic City. A review of the main named subject reveals that there are other SARs from various casinos around the country. This might be indicative of someone laundering large sums of money who is attempting to hide his trail by visiting numerous casinos in several states.

- A SAR might be the result of several SAR submissions by the same institution on the same entity, all of which detail fairly low amounts. When added up, the amount of money in and out rises to a level that now catches your eye. Fortunately, the financial institution has notated that Special Agent Jones from the FBI recently contacted them about the previous SAR written about this particular entity. Before you adopt a case, it would behoove you to reach out to Special Agent Jones and determine whether he has a case that he is actively working. Are there parts of this incident that you and Special Agent Jones would know about that the other does not? Is this something that can be worked jointly?

Other Information Financial Institutions May Provide

Please keep in mind that most specific customer information you receive from a financial institution will come as the result of either a mandatory report filed by the financial institution or a subpoena. Other, cursory information might be obtained via networking at various meetings and seminars (which might lead to a subpoena).

Assuming you have a lead, either from an informant, from result of an arrest, or from a SAR, knowing what type of information is available from the financial institution or from FinCEN is important.

The following is the information available from FinCEN:

- *Suspicious activity reports (SARs)*: SARs are prepared by a financial institution when it believes that activity has occurred that is beyond a reasonable explanation. The report contains customer information such as the name of the financial institution, account number, name of the customer, date of birth, Social Security number (SSN), address, occupation, phone, amount of money involved in the suspicious activity, and narrative description of the activity that the financial institution has deemed to be suspicious. Keep in mind that the subject of the SAR might not be the cat's meow. Be sure to check the names provided in the narrative of the SAR because that might prove more fruitful. A final word on SARs: they are confidential. You can share the information with your boss and the members of your team, and of course the prosecutor, but that's about it. Further, note that most of the financial institution's employees will be unaware of the existence of a SAR because they usually have special units that prepare and submit SARs, and that process is kept confidential even within the institution.

- *Currency transaction reports (CTRs; FinCEN form 112)*: These reports are created whenever a cash transaction over $10,000 is completed (unless the customer has an exemption). For example, a large business, such as a supermarket, may apply for an exemption because they routinely make cash transactions over the $10,000 limit. The CTR contains the name and location of the financial institution, the name of the account holder, the account number, the name of the person making the transaction (for example, it could be an employee of a company), and the amount of the transaction.

- *How can this be helpful:* There is the obvious question, "What is the source of the subject's funds?" Other information might come from connecting the dots such as perhaps the address is familiar and shows up in other reports. Perhaps the subject is a known criminal. By having these on file, it might provide leads about the customer information for later cases. Further, it might provide a law enforcement investigator with a clue as to where a suspect banks when there are no other leads.

- *Form 8300*: This is similar to a CTR in that any cash transaction over $10,000 must be reported. The difference is that Form 8300 is not used by financial institutions. It is a form completed and submitted to FinCEN by trades or businesses. For example, an individual buys a new car from an auto dealership, and he pays for the car in cash. Assuming the price is more than $10,000, the dealership is required to complete and submit Form 8300.

  - *How can this be helpful:* Thinking like a detective, one might ask, why is this subject buying a car with $50,000 cash? Who does that? Most people would use a certified check or some other means of payment. But walking into the dealership with $50,000 in cash is a bit odd. There's nothing wrong with it; it's not illegal, but it does make me question the act. That's what investigation is all about. Perhaps there is a reason for the payment method…legitimate or illegitimate.

- *Foreign bank and financial accounts (FBARs; now called a FinCEN form 114)*: A U.S. resident must file a report of foreign bank and financial accounts report (FBAR) if that person has a financial interest in, signature authority, or other authority over financial accounts in a foreign country and the aggregate value of these accounts exceeds $10,000 at any time during the calendar year.

- *International transportation of currency or monetary instruments (CMIRs; FinCEN form 105)*: Any person who physically transports, mails, or ships currency, travelers checks, or monetary instruments in an aggregate amount over $10,000 into or out of the United States must file a CMIR.

The following is information available from a financial institution:

- *Bank statements*: These include a summary of all transactions of the account during a particular time frame. This is perhaps the best place to begin your investigation.

- *Know your customer information:* All financial institutions are required to ascertain certain basic pedigree information from all customers.

- *Signature cards*: These detail who is allowed to sign on the account. There may be more than one person and even multiple persons if it is a business account. This may provide information on any facilitators or partners in a crime. Further, it provides a sample of the account owner's handwriting.

- *Canceled checks*: Checks deposited and checked written and the information on the back of those checks may provide an abundance of information about additional individuals or entities.

- *Credit cards/debit cards*: This will detail exactly when, where, and how much money was being spent and on what items. Further, as a follow-up step, digital surveillance might be available from a purchase location.

- *Wire transfers*. This will reveal the endpoint, amount, and receiver of the wire transfers.

- *SAR supporting documents*: If the financial institution completed a SAR, then it should have memorialized the results of its internal investigation that led to the decision to file a SAR.

- *Customer contact reports*: Any correspondence between the customer and the financial institution will be noted and saved in the customer's file. This is good to review because a subject's story may change over time.

- *Deposit slips*: This will detail the exact form that money was deposited in. For example, a subject may deposit $10,000, and it would be nice to know that it was all $100 bills or in singles, dimes, and nickels.

- *Money order records*: You can obtain the form that the sender completes, the form completed by the receiver, and any bank drafts drawn by the financial institution to the receiver of the funds.

- *Safe deposit visitation records:* While you cannot look in a safe deposit box without a search warrant, it might be interesting to note how many times an individual visits his safe box. Some banks keep a signature record of the event. Knowing that the subject visits his box once a week and follows that with a wire transfer could prove useful.

Developing the Investigative Mind

A bad guy thinks like a bad guy. He does bad-guy things. He acts like a bad guy. He spends his day trying to think up more bad-guy things to do. He associates with other bad guys who all do more bad-guy things. He goes to the annual bad-guy convention and trade show. He reads *Bad Guy Today* magazine.

One of the advantages of being a bad guy is when a bad guy gets an idea, he can try it immediately, and if it does not work, he can analyze, alter, correct it, and try it again tomorrow—or try something completely different at any time of his choosing. He plays by no rules or regulations, nor does he follow any policies or procedures.

Team Good Guy, however, has an anvil around its neck. First, there is always the issue of the funding dilemma. I'm sure I don't have to remind anyone reading this that prevention usually gets the last bite of the apple. Further, there is the inherent issue that good people tend to think and act like good people. Most of us are not familiar with the bad-guy realm. Advantage: Team Bad Guy.

The usual game plan for Team Good Guy is to fix all known problematic situations. Many times I have heard one of the good guys say something to the effect of, "We have policies that deal with that." Or, "We have top-of-the-line software" or "That has never happened before." However, while you may have policies against the usual suspects, transgressions, incursions, or any known issue, problems still manifest because it is the unknown or future issue that arises. The issue that you are not yet aware of is the most dangerous. Your reference for criteria is effective only on those issues and problems that you already know and is based on good-guy thinking. Just because the good guy cannot think of a problem issue does not mean that the bad guy has not or will not.

Herein lies the crux of a common problem in the land of safety and security. There is a lack of strategic thinking. We usually don't have a unit assigned to play the role of the bad guy (if they even could) other than some basic quality control (which assesses only known problematic situations). I am talking about real strategic thinking that allows a unit to be free thinkers and provides them with the means to truly go outside of the box. Let me provide an example. As all of us in the AML world know, or should know, that a quality AML program usually begins with the customer identification program. That's great, except all subsequent hard AML work goes out the window if the bad guy uses a fictitious ID. Perhaps you believe that you have solved all your worries by implementing a biometric iris scanner.

> Good guy: *"Hey, we finally beat the bad guys; now you can access your account only by putting your eye up to a scanner."*
>
> Bad guy: *"Those fools don't realize that computers operate on a binary system. Everything is reduced to a series of digits on ones and zeros. If we hack into their system and infiltrate the code system, then we will have everyone's iris identifiers, and we can become them...cool."*

It's always a matter of preparing for the unknown. I remember going through the State Police Academy many moons ago and some old crusty sergeant once said to me, "Son, you don't know what you don't know." Boy, was he ever right!

Now you may say, let's hire some bad guys to get their input. I am not a fan of this concept. I would rather hire the investigator who arrested the bad guy or the attorney who prosecuted him. Admittedly, there may be some advantages to consulting with a bad guy. However, I would hesitate to give him the keys to the kingdom. Some may say that the former bad guy has paid his dues and has seen the light; that might be so. But I will remind you that he usually is remorseful only because he got caught. Not too many bad guys, particularly white-collar criminals, have walked into the front door of the police station and said, "Here I am, and I'm sorry for what I have done. I surrender, and I'd like to make it up to society by working for the good guys now." Furthermore, that mind-set, the "let's give the bad guy a chance" mind-set, flies in the face of my number-one rule: be suspicious. This is exactly the mind-set I am talking about. Being forgiving works well in church; being suspicious works better in risk assessment.

Tip
Remain suspicious of former bad guys. Being forgiving works well in church; being suspicious works better in risk assessment.

Let's move past the "let's hire a bad guy" idea and focus more on the mind-set of the good guys. First, be inquisitive. It's OK to be suspicious. Don't get so hung up on political correctness that you don't do your job. You are being paid to be suspicious if you are a financial institution investigator, analyst, detective, or special agent. As long as you can justify your position, you are OK. If you are writing a SAR for a financial institution, you have "safe harbor" and don't have to worry about repercussions for filing a SAR. Follow through on your uneasiness. If you are not the person who takes things further, then escalate the situation to someone who does. If an incident makes the hair on the back of your neck stand up, then by all means, take this further.

To help someone become more inquisitive, you can help them know where to turn. A friend of mine who runs the AML division at a large bank does something progressive. He has his staff spend some time each day exploring the Internet—going to new sites, clicking various advanced setting buttons, and generally becoming more aware of the Internet and its sources of information. The rewards surface when enhanced due diligence is required, and the staff can navigate to where they need to go quicker and with more accuracy. This concept works for financial institutions, regulators, and law enforcement.

"The temptation to form premature theories upon insufficient data is the bane of our profession."
Sherlock Holmes

Use Your Instincts

A key piece of advice in law enforcement and financial investigations is to use your instincts. Good instincts are part of developing the investigative mind. Your instincts come from your environment, experience, knowledge, and ability. We are not born with investigative instincts; they are developed. As I mentioned earlier, good people think like good people. This is why I sometimes bang my head against the desk when I read some of the AML blogs or listservs where it appears that certain people or entities that are being investigated are given the benefit of the doubt; excuses are even being created for them by the people who are assigned the task of investigating them. Stop right there! It is not your job, nor mine, to determine guilt or innocence. It is our jobs to obtain the facts and report them. When we don't have all the facts (and you usually don't), you make use of all your instincts. While instincts have no place in the court of law, they sure should take front and center while you are completing an investigation. The more experience and knowledge you have, usually the greater your instincts. Follow your instincts, go through doors, open windows, turn over stones, but find as many of the facts as you can without predisposition or prejudice. If something does not feel right, then try to figure out why. Be suspicious, yet judge slowly.

Tip
Be suspicious, yet judge slowly.

Tips for Developing the Investigative Mind

Here are some thoughts on developing your investigative mind:

- *Be suspicious, be suspicious, be suspicious*: The case has come across your desk for a reason. Somebody or some software has viewed this case as unusual or odd. It is up to the investigator to review, analyze, research, investigate, and then report. We all understand a person is innocent until proven guilty. However, this is not the court of law. I'm suspicious of everyone, at least until I can confidently cross them off my list. I cross them off by completing a thorough investigation, not by guessing, assuming, or being captivated by their nice smile. Remember, bad guys try to look and act like good guys. I'm sure there are some who might feel that this is a terrible way to live. I'm not suggesting that you live your life suspicious of everyone all the time. I turn it off. Well, hmmm…OK, so maybe I don't; that's a bad example. But you can turn if off when you leave the office. Being like Aunt Bea from Mayberry (Andy Griffith reference there… showing my age) is just not good enough if you want to be a top-of-the-line investigator. The investigator's job is to discover the facts as best as possible. Each case should be approached with suspicion on the mind but with neutrality and evenhandedness as your course of action.

- *Employ the smell test*: If you think it stinks, it probably does. You do this job every day, and you work with people who do this job every day. If for some reason the hair on the back of your neck is standing up, then go with the feeling. You are probably right. Understand, of course, that hair standing up on the back of your neck is not a valid probable cause in the court of law, so you do need to be able to articulate your feelings. What is making you feel this way? Figure that out and then run with it. This goes back to instincts. Don't be too quick to dismiss your gut feelings. If you can't figure it out, ask a new set of eyes to take a look. Don't be embarrassed to ask. I have yet to meet anyone who resembled Sherlock Holmes and has all the answers. We can all use a little assistance from time to time.

- *Consider many hypotheses*: The investigator must understand that if he considers only one hypothesis, then he is may be missing the boat. You must begin the case entertaining numerous possible hypotheses. The more knowledge you have about current trends and patterns, then the more hypotheses become available. Keeping up with the latest and greatest techniques and methods is important.

Make available new sources of information or technology. This might be more difficult because it usually involves spending budget money. However, there are other things that you can avail yourself of, such as local meetings with your peers and law enforcement, various free seminars and webinars, or trade magazines and publications.

Never say, "There has never been any cases before like this," or "No one has been arrested for this type of activity previously." Ahhh, the call of the mild! I hear this all the time from people who aren't in law enforcement. Hey gang, just because you don't know of any cases does not mean that law enforcement is not currently engaged in one. How would you like to be the first one victimized? Did you ever notice whenever some nutcase goes on a shooting spree, the TV news interviews the neighbors and they always say the same thing—"He was such a nice guy; we never knew of any problems." You are not being paid to be the clueless neighbor; you are being paid to keep the place secure. Your job should be to envision the possibilities and create a path of action to prevent disaster. Refer to the first rule.

- *Be guided by JADE—justify, articulate, and define everything*: Assuming that you no longer believe in fairy dust and unicorns and have morphed into the "I'm suspicious of everything that moves attitude," then you need to follow the JADE rule. In an investigation, everything you do is memorialized. You never know where that file will end up—executive board, law enforcement, or courtroom. You have to justify all your actions and further articulate and explain why you did what you did or why you did not do what you did not do. Your results will be defined, and ultimately an action will be taken. (Note that even an inaction needs to be defined.)

I am sure that having a law enforcement background certainly helps with the "suspicious mind-set." But that does not mean you have to be retired law enforcement to work in the compliance field. All it takes is not working like the other units where customer service is paramount. The AML or fraud side of the house was created to look into the activity of those same customers and decide whether there is anything fishy going on. That is tough to do if you more concerned about a happy customer. Be professional at all times and be curious. It's OK; it's your job.

How I Got Here

As I noted earlier, I will spend a few moments on how I got from point A to where I am now, writing this book. I am a bit hesitant to talk about this because I think it's borderline vain, but I get asked about this—a lot. So, if this helps someone just starting out or thinking about going in this direction, then I think it is worth it to discuss this.

While working in one of the New York State Police Bureau of Criminal Investigation (BCI) squads, we were getting a lot of credit card and check fraud cases. Additionally, this was the beginning of the Internet era, and identity theft crimes were just beginning. Furthermore, on a personal note, I realized that having a skill that not many others possessed would come in handy. Until I started to catch a lot of the credit card cases and a couple of other large fraud cases, I had no idea what direction I would have to take to find my specific field of expertise. When it became obvious to me when no one else in the squad showed much interest in financial crimes, I started to grab those cases.

At about this time, I was researching financial crimes investigations and discovered a group called the Association of Certified Fraud Examiners. For a couple of bucks a year I could obtain membership and would get a monthly magazine (*Fraud* magazine) that spoke about the subjects that I was now interested in. Further, the ACFE offered classes and seminars on financial crime topics. The funding for joining the association and/or attending and seminars or conferences came out of my own pocket because there was no way that the job would pay the fees for me. This was the first of a series of conscious decisions to spend my own money to educate myself and create a skill that not too many had. This seems to be a hurdle that many have an issue with. While I completely agree that the job should be funding these training and educational sessions, let's get real. That was just not going to happen. Law enforcement has a limited budget and sending someone to these classes was not going to even be considered. It was quite annoying when I would attend a class and most of the other people in the class were getting the class funded by their private employer…but so be it, I knew what I was getting into when I signed up with law enforcement so I can't complain. Now back to the timeline. Catching the credit card cases was the opening of the door for me, and electing to spend my own time and money educating myself was me walking through the door.

> **Tip**
> Invest in yourself. If you think a class, seminar, magazine, or similar would be useful in your career, then seriously consider spending your own money. Rest assured the investment will return dividends over time.

I eventually stumbled upon a fraud case that seemed to get bigger and bigger every day. From my contacts at various banks I learned that one of the local FBI agents was also looking into the same entity. We both had pieces of the puzzle that the other did not have. Subsequently this case turned into something much bigger, and I became part of an FBI-led white-collar crimes task force. This gave me additional experience and knowledge and further opened my eyes to several things: what was needed to conduct these types of investigations and the realization that I actually enjoyed this side of the house.

At this time, I had been considering going back to school for a master's degree. My law enforcement job actually did have a program, if accepted, that would allow a discounted price for a master's degree in public administration. However, this did not particularly serve me any great purpose because that was not the field of my interest and not the field that would provide me a specialty. I chose instead to attend a program at Utica College of Syracuse University that would provide me with a master's degree in economic crime management. That was definitely hitting the nail on the head. The only problem was, the nail was going to cost me a bundle. My decision was to suck it up and invest in my own future. It was a two-year program that was mostly completed online but required a residency three weeks each year. This was vacation time that I had to take to complete this residency requirement and a hotel bill for staying near the school. That hurt too, but I made a commitment to carve out a niche for myself, and this was the only way I could see doing that.

Just about the time that I was going to graduate from the master's program, the state police decided to create an official financial crimes unit. This was going to be a team of one…at least for starters. I applied, but unfortunately I did not get the position. It was given to someone who the bosses at headquarters were a little more familiar with. Hey, that's the way things roll. While disappointed, I bore no ill-will toward the guy who got the gig. He subsequently turned out to be a really good guy, and we became friends. While I did not get that post, a few months later I got a call from one the big bosses who had interviewed me for the financial crimes position. He said there was a new multi-agency task force opening in Manhattan and asked if I would be interested in taking the position. I said, "How much time do I have to decide?" He said, "Until I hang up this phone." I said, "I'll take it!" Fortunately for me, the boss remembered me from the initial interview for the financial crimes unit and thought I would be good for this detail. All my extra efforts were starting to pay off.

After arriving at the El Dorado High Intensity Financial Crimes Area Task Force, I met up with agents from the Secret Service, FBI, DEA, Customs (now ICE), IRS, Postal Inspection, NYPD, Manhattan District Attorney's Office,

FinCEN, and New York State Banking Department, along with a few other agencies that were in and out of the task force at various times. Most all of the cases were related to organized crime (until a few jackasses flew planes into buildings and changed everything). The learning curve was a straight line upward. I was fascinated and having a blast. Part of our mission was communicating with financial institutions, and that was a whole new set of criteria that I needed to learn. Financial institutions had a different playbook than law enforcement, and if I wanted to be in this job, I needed to understand financial institutions and regulators. It helped being in Manhattan, the financial capital of the world, because there was much opportunity to meet up with all these newfound friends, bankers, and regulators.

We had several regular meetings on both the money laundering and fraud sides (External Fraud group and HIFCA AML meetings to name two). Back in those days, it was a pre-financial intelligence unit era—meaning the banks had their fraud side and their AML units and usually never the two did meet. That made absolutely no sense to us because we knew that it was the same bad guys who were committing the predicate crimes, such as fraud, that ultimately had to launder the proceeds from those crimes. So, why would financial institutions separate the two? It drove us crazy, but fortunately after much discussion with the financial institutions and regulators, the FIU concept began to see the light of day.

One thing nice about working at a federal-led task force was that they had money for training. Many of us went to the Federal Law Enforcement Training Center (FLECC) in Georgia; sometimes trainers would come to us, and occasionally we had funds to send a few people to seminars and workshops. I went to numerous seminars on their dime and on my own dime, again with the thinking that I was investing in my own future. Out of one of these larger seminars an association was born. It was called the Association of Certified Money Laundering Specialists (ACAMS). The membership was mostly financial institutions, but it had a few law enforcement representatives. I attended as many of the seminars as possible; most I paid for, but some were paid by the feds. This association created its own certification program. I saw the value of this right from the get-go. I subsequently went on to be the co-chair of the first chapter of ACAMS. That put me in a position where many people in the industry knew me, and I could get things done either by the book or just by picking up the phone and calling the right person. The next thing I knew was that I was getting phone calls about speaking at various seminars on whatever hot topic was occurring. All the hard work was definitely paying off.

There are still other associations out there that help educate, such as

International Association of Financial Crimes Investigators (IAFCI). Seminars are also provided by the American Banking Association (ABA), the Federal Reserve, the District Attorney's Office, third-party vendors, and big-name financial institutions. They are out there if you are willing to search and put up the bucks.

I did not stop with the learning process and continued with various schools, seminars, and webinars. Further, there is plenty of information available via a number of web sites; some are pay-for sites, and some are free. To this day I still attend a number of antimoney-laundering events. Because money-laundering methods are always changing, adapting, and improving, it is imperative that we keep up. Whenever you think you know it all, you become vulnerable.

So, in summation, my takeaway message is that you should not be afraid or unwilling to spend your own time and money on your own education. No one can ever take away your education, and sooner or later it will come in handy. And for those who are curious, I had numerous offers for AML jobs in the private world before I retired from law enforcement (and still do). AML is a booming industry, and my timing was lucky, but my resume was no luck. I busted my hump to get an education and various certifications and work in one of the largest money-laundering task forces in the world. So, if you put the effort in, you too should be able to reap the rewards.

Summary

There is no doubt in my mind that law enforcement's presence with financial crimes is growing. The vast majority of crimes are committed for greed, and the vast majority of those crimes are commited by some form of organized criminal element. It makes sense that law enforcement would adopt a "cut the head off of the snake" approach. In other words, why go after the little guy when you can get the kingpin. To go after the kingpin, then a "follow the money" approach should apply. These cases are time consuming but well worth it if an entire criminal organization is brought down. It is interesting to observe the entire chain of investigators in case; from the bank investigator through law enforcement to prosecution. Each one is very important to the outcome.

Sometimes the financial institution investigator can become disenchanted as he does a lot of work, passes it along to law enforcement and never hears another thing about that case again. Never finding out what happened. Sometimes never even knowing if his institution competed a SAR, or if law enforcement ever got involved and if so to what extent. I think weall need to remember this investigator. Without him/her, there may not be any escalation. While it may not be possible to detail any further information about the incident, I do think it's important that the front line investigator at the financial institution gets some form of acknowledgement. A slap on the back, or an atta-boy would go a long way to keep the interest of that front line investigator.

Next up we will discuss some foreign policies that all AML personal should be aware of. Seeing how we have a global economy it becomes imperitive to understand the nuances of various laundering issues around the world.

8. International Standards

The Importance of a Global Approach to Money Laundering

⊠

(1)

There are many guidelines, measures, and specifications created by numerous organizations and associations to assist in the anti-money laundering (AML) arena. Many are geared to the overall AML regime of a particular country. Each has its own unique mission and purpose.

You might wonder, "Why is it important to understand international standards in AML?" That's a fair question. The fair answer is that money laundering is a global concern. Organized criminal enterprises are transnational and do not recognize borders. In fact, they use international borders as a viable method to fly below the AML radar. While the U.S. dollar is still the world's economic reserve currency, it does not mean that we should be concerned only with the U.S. Bank Secrecy Act. Do banks in the United States conduct business globally? Are there customers with business or addresses outside of the United States? Do companies require correspondent banking? Do they require payable-through accounts?[1]

The answer to each question is an unequivocal *yes*. That's why even small community banks should be concerned about globalization. Money laundering is not just a U.S. problem. It is an issue that affects everyone, and the best way to deter, detect, and prevent money laundering is through a unified global effort.

Various Organizations That Create Guidelines

While the United States has the benefit of the Bank Secrecy Act (BSA), there are many countries around the globe that have no AML policies/laws or have limited ones. Several organizations exist to assist the global financial community in creating, developing, updating, and maintaining an AML position. The following sections discuss several of these organizations.

The Financial Action Task Force

The Financial Action Task Force (FATF) is a Paris-based membership association made up of various countries. Currently, there are 34 member counties, 2 regional bodies, and 29 regional associate members (*observers*). Each member country has representation within the ranks. In the United States, the lead authority in the FATF delegation is the U.S. Department of the Treasury.

FATF meets three times per year. One of its goals is to create a multigovernment AML and counterterrorist financing (CTF) policy and procedures guideline, something that would be implemented at the national and global levels. The concept is that since money laundering is a global problem, we need to have a reasonably unified approach for nations to combat the issues. The FATF 40 provides such an outline. This is not a binding document, and member nations may not follow all the suggestions in totality; member nations, however, should be generally compliant with the recommendations.

The FATF 40 is a detailed list of 40 recommendations to establish and maintain a certain standard for a country's AML policy. (In the United States, something quite similar would be the Bank Secrecy Act.) Some recommendations deal with the following issues:

- Money laundering and confiscation
- Terrorist financing
- Preventative measures
- Transparency and beneficial ownership
- Powers and responsibilities of competent authorities
- International cooperation

The FATF 40 was created in 1989, and FATF has revised and updated its recommendations several times since inception.

The FATF 40 has become the FATF 40 + 9. The update came after the attacks of September 11, 2001, and it presented an additional 8 recommendations that specifically dealt with terrorist financing. Subsequently, an additional 9th recommendation was added; together, the 9 recommendations provide special guidelines on terrorist financing.

To assist with implementation of the 40 + 9 recommendations, FATF produces a series of white papers on numerous topics of money-laundering concern, including the latest money-laundering techniques and technologies. Additionally, its web site is full of information (see www.fatf-gafi.org).

Tip

Head to www.fatf-gafi.org for more information on the FATF 40 + 9. Further, anyone who is in the AML field should bookmark this web site.

Additionally, FATF has associate members that could be viewed as "local chapters." These associate members mostly abide by FATF 40 + 9, but they also may include some specific regional issues in their policies. The following are some of these associate members:

- Asia/Pacific Group
- Caribbean Financial Action Task Force
- Eurasian Group
- Eastern and Southern Africa AML Group
- Financial Action Task Force of Latin America
- Inter Governmental Action Group of West Africa
- Middle East and North Africa FATF

There are a number of international organizations (such as Basel, Egmont, IMF, Interpol, and the United Nations) that have observer status in FATF.

FATF also provides for an annual self-assessment and peer review. Based upon evaluation from the member nations, specifically the International Cooperation Review Group, the review may identify jurisdictions that have strategic AML/CFT deficiencies. Countries identified as such are placed on the High Risk and Non-Cooperative Jurisdictions list. That list is sometimes referred to as the *name and shame list*. FATF will assist any of these jurisdictions with rectifying and coordinating countermeasures to bring the nation into compliance with the minimum standard for AML/CFT.

Basel Committee on Banking Supervision

The Basel Committee on Banking Supervision was developed in 1974 and is a subgroup of the Bank for International Settlements (BIS). The BIS has 60 member central banks representing various countries globally. The Basel Committee on Banking Supervision provides a forum for cooperation on banking supervisory issues such as regulations, supervision, and the practices of banks globally to enhance financial stability. The Basel Committee is located in Basel, Switzerland, where the members meet four times per year. They are central supervising banks. (The U.S. central supervising bank is the Federal Reserve.) Much like the FATF 40, the BIS makes suggestions and creates guidelines. There are no legally binding documents, nor does it possess any legislative authority. However, it strongly and successfully encourages general cooperation among countries.

One of the Bank for International Settlements' major concerns is cross-jurisdictional or correspondent banking. Initially, Basel was to make sure that all foreign banks would have a consistent standard set of supervisory standards. The Basel Committee has come out with several papers, most notably "Core Principles for Effective Banking Supervision" and "The Supervision of Cross Border Banking." The papers mention how important having sound know your customer and customer due diligence policies are, particularly in a corresponding/respondent banking relationship.

Tip

Know your customer (KYC) and customer identification programs (CIPs) are important because they provide the greatest possibility of detecting and deterring the money-laundering threat simply by understanding exactly who the customer is and if the activity and transactions make sense. In a correspondent relationship, all of the KYC and CIP activities fall upon the respondent bank. The concern is whether the respondent bank has fulfilled its obligation to KYC and CIP.

Additionally noted is the need to not only establish the identity of the customer but also the importance of monitoring account activity. The paper describes the four key elements of asound KYC policy.

- *Customer identification*: Procedures should be in place that will allow the financial institution to verify the identity of a customer, both at the onset of the relationship and if a significant transaction occurs or there is a major change in the way the account is used by the customer.

- *Risk management*: The financial institution's board of directors should be fully immersed in establishing and maintaining appropriate AML measures.

- *Customer acceptance*: A risk assessment should be developed that includes a matrix of risk indicators surrounding a customer that can help determine the risk level of the account.

- *Monitoring*: Determining the normal and usual account activity of a customer and then identifying activity that occurs outside of the regular pattern.

While the aforementioned concepts are noted by the Basel Committee on Banking Supervision, which is bank-focused, many other nonbank financial institutions have adopted similar policies. Therefore, the concepts should not be limited to the banking community. I strongly believe that nonbank financial institutions and professional intermediaries (gatekeepers) should also be subject to arduous customer due diligence standards.

Wolfsberg

Wolfsberg is an association of 11 global banks with the concept of developing industry standards and helping shape guidelines for banks and regulators. It started out addressing money-laundering risks in the world of private banking. In 1999, at Chateau Wolfsberg in Switzerland, it began to construct the draft for private banking AML guidelines. Subsequently, Wolfsberg has published numerous papers with reference to various money-laundering topics.[2] Perhaps best-known are the following papers:

- "AML Principles for Private Banking"
- "AML Principals for Correspondent Banking"
- "Beneficial Ownership"
- "AntiCorruption"
- "AML Questionnaire"

Its template called "Questionnaire for Correspondent Banking" has become an industry standard for onboarding any new respondent banks.

The wolfsburg eleven

- Banco Santander
- Bank of Tokyo-Mitsubishi
- Barclays

- Citigroup
- Credit Suisse
- Deutsche Bank
- Goldman Sachs
- HSBC
- J.P. Morgan Chase
- Societe Generale
- UBS

Additionally, Wolfsberg maintains close watch on new techniques and the latest in various money-laundering methods—such as stored value cards.

An interesting addition to Wolfsberg is the International Registry. This is a due-diligence repository for intelligence purposes. It maintains information on each financial institution's pertinent documents, such as licenses and articles of incorporation. The purpose is to eliminate the need to complete repetitive tasks, such as ascertaining each financial institution's pedigree documents. This is extremely helpful in the corresponding banking and counterparty research areas.

Similar to the Basel Committee, Wolfsberg has no legal or legislative authority. The member banks meet quarterly, and there are no rules of discipline.

Once again, I suggest that anyone in the AML field should also have the web site of the Wolfsberg Group (www.wolfsberg-principles.com) bookmarked on their computer.

Egmont

The financial intelligence units of various countries (in the United States, that would be FinCEN) first met at Egmont Arenberg Palace in Brussels, Belgium, in 1995. Its mission was simply to establish an informal method of international cooperation. (As FATF recommends, each country should develop and maintain a financial intelligence unit.) The goal was to figure out a way for information to be shared. If you consider that many organized criminal enterprises are transnational, it only makes sense that the good guys should have a way to communicate and share intelligence in a cross-border context. This concept is important because the law enforcement community in country A has no legal authority in country B. A subpoena or search warrant would have no legal merit in a foreign jurisdiction. Therefore, assistance with intelligence gathering may be conducted via a reciprocal method from one financial intelligence unit (of a country) to another. This should happen without any uneccesary delay or without undue restrictions being placed on the information.

Over the years the membership has grown to 139 member nations. Egmont addressed the issues of not only sharing information with law enforcement and regulators but also creating and maintaining an effective platform for that exchange of information to occur and to develop new and additional effective financial intelligence units.

Definition
A financial intelligence unit (FIU) is a central, national agency responsible for receiving, analyzing, and disseminating financial information to the competent authorities.

European Union

The European directive is the rule of law in Europe, first adopted in 1991. Unlike the previously mentioned standards, the EU financial regulations have the full weight of law behind them. The EU's goal is to protect the financial system from money laundering and terrorist financing. It is a version of the U.S. Bank Secrecy Act. To date, there have been three directives relating to anti-money laundering issued over the course of 23 years, but in the very near future a fourth directive will be established (called the 4th EU Directive on Money Laundering). The 1st Directive strictly discussed drug trafficking. The 2nd Directive broadened the scope by including all serious crimes as predicate[3] crimes and not just drug trafficking. The 3rd EU Directive brought terrorist financing to light. Each directive subsequently updated the previous directive.[4] The current directives require the following:

- Conducting due-diligence checks prior to onboarding a new customer at a financial institution
- Gathering and maintaining ID documents
- Defining money laundering for legal purposes
- Adding money service businesses to covered institutions
- Including lawyers in the scope of directive

Note

Lawyers in the United States are not required to maintain AML polices.

- Extending reporting requirements to transactions over 15,000 euros
- Ensuring institutions take a risk-based approach to customer due diligence
- Monitoring politically exposed persons (PEPS) and their close associates

The EU directiveis similar in fashion to the US. Bank Secrecy Act and, in turn, the FATF 40 + 9. There are differences, of course, because it would be impossible for the entire globe to accommodate one rule of law. However, the similarities are much greater than the differences. The EU directives are law and as such are binding, meaning this document is not just a suggestion or a guideline such as Wolfsberg, Basel, or FATF.

International Monetary Fund

The International Monetary Fund (IMF)[5] is an organization consisting of 188 countries concerned about the integrity and stability of the legitimate financial community and the economy in general. It provides assistance on policies and procedures to member nations that are economically distressed, and it assists developing countries in achieving economic standards.

The IMF has been incorporating AML concepts into its procedures since February 2001 by disseminating papers such as "Financial System Abuse, Financial Crime and Money Laundering."[6] It also approaches its AML campaign with a focus on anticorruption programs. Before it will assist any developing nation with financial help, the IMF insists on the application of international AML standards.

In 2006, the IMF published a manual called "The World Bank Reference Guide."[7] Besides providing a good basic money-laundering primer, it also details AML and the CFT framework for a country. It is, in its own words, a "step-by-step approach to achieve compliance with international standards."

So, why should you care about international standards? Money laundering is a global issue. The proceeds of crime will flow in and out of numerous countries and various financial institutions large and small. Unfortunately, there is no safe corner of the world that bad guys will not abuse. It would behoove you to be aware of the dynamics of your global partners and policies of any geographics that a customer might take advantage of.

Transparency International

Transparency International[8] is a nongovernment entity based in Berlin, Germany, with offices in more than 100 countries. Transparency International takes a stance against corruption. It believes in transparency, accountability, and integrity at all levels and in public and private service.

Where there is corruption, there is money laundering. Transparency International provides a helpful tool called the Corruption Perception Index (CPI). This comes in handy when performing due diligence and attempting to risk rate a customer or prospective customer. The CPI measures the perceived levels of public-sector corruption in 175 countries and territories. Hence, a country with a low score on the CPI may then be issued a higher risk rating. For example, Somalia, which has a CPI of 8 out of 100 and is last on the list, should certainly attract attention on any risk assessment. (For those who must know, number-one is Denmark, as of this writing.) Transparency International is not an AML policy maker, its recommendations do not carry the weight of law, and they are not government-binding; however, Transparency International provides an excellent source of intelligence that should provide a heads-up to any possible money-laundering activity.

Economic Sanctions

Economic sanctions are actions, such as trade restrictions and diminished commercial activity, taken by countries against other countries, entities, individuals, or vessels strictly for political reasons. Those underlying reasons might well be various forms of organized criminal enterprises and money launderers. Organizations that make use of sanctions include the U.K. Treasury Office, U.S. Office of Foreign Asset Control, European Union, Hong Kong Monetary Authority, and the United Nations.

Usually a sanction is created to punish or to attempt to have the sanctionee change their ways or submit to the thinking or methods of the sanctioning country. Sanctions are not universally implemented, and they are effective only by the country that establishes them. Each country may establish its own sanctions against a common subject. However, many of the sanctions have a United Nations nexus and may include similar mandates from other governments.

Let's use the U.S. Office of Foreign Asset Control (OFAC) to explain how sanctions work. OFAC is a division of the Department of the Treasury. It issues and enforces economic and trade sanctions based upon U.S. foreign policy. The target of those policies are foreign countries and regimes, narcotic traffickers, terrorist organizations, anyone related to the proliferation of weapons of mass destruction, and any other national security threats.

Additionally, financial institutions outside of the United States must abide by the OFAC-issued sanctions if there is any correspondent relationship between a U.S. bank and a foreign bank or the foreign bank settles international payments using a U.S.-dollar clearing account.

OFAC will not allow transactions to be completed for people or organizations whose names are on one of OFAC lists, and it requires that their assets be blocked. An individual, group, vessel, or entity that appears on an OFAC list (the SDN list) is called a *specially designated national*.

It is important to note that many circumstances have their exceptions. It is possible to have dealings with a regime that has been sanctioned. Events may occur requiring financial transactions. An example might be those dealing with a natural disaster in a country that has total comprehensive sanctions. It would be possible to request a special and limited OFAC license to provide certain goods or services for that country. A major earthquake in Sudan may prompt an organization such as the American Red Cross to request a special permit to help administer humanitarian aid.

As an outsider looking at the OFAC program, it may on the surface appear to be a black-or-white issue. Either a name is on a list or not. Full sanctions or partial sanctions. That's pretty simple. However, I can assure you that it is rarely that simple. More often than not, a particular individual or entity has all sorts of tentacles and may not directly cross the line but do so indirectly. For example, a customer who owns a company in the United States has their product, made in Hong Kong, put onto a vessel for delivery to Italy. The vessel is flagged in Denmark. That all sounds good, and no sanctioned countries are involved. However, it is discovered that the vessel is making a stop in North Korea. That would put the kibosh on allowing the transaction to take place because a sanctioned country is touching part of this transaction (even though it has nothing to do with the customer or the product).

As a financial institution, dealingwith sanctions is a must. It can become quite intense and confusing. For this reason, most of the larger financial institutions have their own sanctions unit within the institution. In the past, several financial institutions neglected their sanctions obligations and allowed transactions to continue to countries or entities that were designated as primary money-laundering concerns and under OFAC sanctions. Those institutions were discovered and have paid a hefty price in both regulatory fines and remediation costs, not to mention the reputational damage when the media discovers that a financial institution is dealing with sanctioned country. What would the media say if, as a result of a financial institution's disregard for sanctions, a terrorist event is funded?

Types of sanctions programs

Comprehensive Programs Prohibits all exports, imports, financing, trade, brokering, facilitation, and all commercial activity. Countries affected include Cuba, Iran, Sudan, and Syria.

    Limited Programs Prohibitions vary based on program; countries include Myanmar, North Korea, and Ukraine.

    Activity-Based Programs Prohibits transactions involving an interest with an individual, entity, or vessel appearing on the OFAC SND list based on certain activities. Categories include narcotics trafficking, terrorism, and transnational organized crime.

    Regime Based Programs Prohibits transactions based on an interest with an individual, entity, or vessel appearing on the OFAC SDN list depending on governmental involvement.

I have sat with many bankers assigned to their sanctions unit (many of them who formally worked at OFAC in Washington, D.C.), and I have always been truly amazed at the amount of information that they must look at when dealing with sanction issues. It is definitely not as simple as it may appear. Furthermore, there is little room for error. Banks have been subject to numerous fines for various OFAC violations. Most violations are oversights, but some involved wire stripping—deliberately removing any names or information that might be on a sanction list so as to allow the transaction to take place.

I have come to the conclusion that whenever there is a possible sanction issue, do yourself a favor and call the OFAC team in your institution. The lists are constantly changing, and rules are being updated in a blink of an eye. Let the people who deal with this stuff on an everyday basis provide you with the proper guidance. Those of you who work for a small financial institution...well, on the bright side, you probably don't or have limited engagement in international banking activities or international trade. On the dark side, it does mean that you probably don't have an OFAC team and that you are wearing the OFAC hat all by yourself. Ideally, you have some decent software solutions that will help, but chances are, you've got nothing. Fortunately, all the various sanctioned lists and SDNs are available for free from the OFAC website.[9] This might be more time-consuming than if you had specific software, but you should be able to find your answers there.

USA PATRIOT ACT

The U.S. Congress passed the USA PATRIOT ACT in 2001 as a result of the terrorist attacks of 9/11. The USA PATRIOT ACT strengthened and bolstered the Bank Secrecy Act to respond to the greater threat from terrorism. At this point, you may be asking yourself, "What is the USA PATRIOT ACT doing in an international section?" Good question. The answer is that the USA PATRIOT ACT has extraterritorial impact. There are many non-U.S. institutions that perform business in the United States (in other words, corresponding banking relationships).

While there are many provisions of the USA PATRIOT ACT, I will only discuss those sections that may have international consequences.

Section 311

Special Measures for Jurisdictions, Financial Institutions or International Transactions of Primary Money Laundering Concern

This section provides the United States with the ability to deem a country or financial institution a primary money-laundering concern. This means that the United States can require U.S. banks to stop any relationship that they may have with the particular named area of concern or provide specific information about the subject of concern. The possible required acts are as follows:

- Providing additional records and KYC details on the owners of the accounts in question
- Providing information on beneficial ownership
- Gathering information on payable-through accounts
- Further information on correspondent accounts
- Exiting or placing specific conditions on certain correspondent or payable-through accounts

Section 312

Special Due Diligence for Correspondent Accounts and Private Banking Accounts

This section requires enhanced due diligence (EDD) with reference to correspondent accounts maintained for a foreign financial institution and for private banking accounts established for non-U.S. people. Determining whether the account is owned by a PEP is of major concern. (Private banking accounts are usually defined as an account with a minimum aggregate deposit of $1 million, and a bank employee is assigned to that account.)

Section 313
Prohibition on U.S. Correspondent Accounts with Foreign Shell Banks

This section prevents financial institutions from establishing, maintaining, administering, or managing correspondent accounts in the United States for, or on behalf of, a foreign shell bank. Additionally, they are mandated to take reasonable actions to make sure that their correspondent accounts are not used to indirectly provide correspondent services to a shell bank.

Definition
Shell bank—A bank that does not have a physical presence in the country in which it was incorporated and licensed. Further, it is unaffiliated with any regulated financial group. In other words, there is no actual bank; it might be a post office box.

Section 319
Forfeiture from U.S. Correspondent Accounts for Foreign Banks

319(a) allows for the forfeiture from U.S. correspondent accounts when funds have been deposited with a foreign bank. The U.S. government is not required to trace the funds originally deposited in the foreign bank.

319(b) allows the U.S. Attorney General or the Secretary of the Treasury to issue a summons or subpoena to any foreign bank that maintains a correspondent account in the United States. Additionally, any request from a U.S. regulator or federal law enforcement office related to those accounts are to be produced within 120 hours.

The USA PATRIOT ACT's anti-money laundering provisions were created to help detect and detour entities that would try to launder and integrate their illegal proceeds into the legitimate financial system. Bad guys need to continue the cycle of crime, then launder, then more crime. The provisions of the USA

PATRIOT ACT assist in preventing the bad guys from exploiting the legitimate financial system and ideally preventing them from committing more crimes. The USA PATRIOT ACT, which is part of the Bank Secrecy Act, is the crux of U.S. AML efforts. Anyone in the AML industry in the United States should be keenly aware of the rules of the USA PATRIOT ACT and how the various laws apply to their institution and situation.

Summary

There are so many parts of the AML wheel. From a distance, it seems like it would be easy: just learn a few rules and you're off and running, but not so. In all the years I've been involved with money laundering, I have yet to meet anyone who is an expert in every part of the money-laundering battle. However, it is certainly possible to become knowledgeable and have a functional awareness about many areas of AML. It might be tough at first to comprehend why the various global standards are important. Money laundering is not just a local or domestic issue; it is a global issue. Your total comprehension of the overall money-laundering dilemma becomes greater once you understand the global consequences.

We have been building up our AML knowledge, and next up will be a chapter on the convergence of fraud and anti-money laundering. As was mentioned earlier, there has to be a predicate crime to bring about the charges of money laundering. One of those charges is some type of fraud. Financial institutions usually have a separate fraud unit, but there is a lot of overlap between fraud and AML. This is why I will discuss in the next chapter the convergence of fraud and anti-money laundering.

Footnotes

1 *Payable-through account*: A form of a correspondent account where a domestic financial institution allows customers of its foreign corresponding bank (respondent bank) to have access to the U.S. banking system. In other words, those foreign customers can write checks and make deposits at the U.S. bank just like any local customer. The AML risk is heightened because of a potential lack of due diligence conducted on the foreign customer by the respondent bank.

2 www.wolfsberg-principles.com/standards.html

3 *Predicate crime*: The criminal act that must be committed to give rise to the prosecution of money laundering (also referred to as the specified unlawful activity). Examples are drug trafficking, arms dealing, illegal gambling, and so on.

4 http://eur-lex.europa.eu/legal-content/EN/TXT/PDF/?uri=CELEX:32005L0060&from=EN

5 www.IMF.org

6 www.imf.org/external/publications/pubindadv.html

7 www1.worldbank.org/finance/html/comprehensive_reference:guide__0.html

8 https://www.transparency.de

9 https://sdnsearch.ofac.treas.gov

9. Fraud and Anti-money Laundering

The New Financial Crime Model

✉

(1)

A credit card theft ring has been operating in the area of Brooklyn, New York. They have been involved in skimming credit cards at various gas stations, restaurants, and retail merchants. A sharp fraud investigator working for one of the banks whose credit card has been compromised notices a trend that indicates possible locations of a number of the breeches. Ultimately, a suspicious activity report (SAR) is completed and submitted.

An anti-money laundering (AML) investigator from the same bank observes numerous red-flag transactions that resulted in several "alerts" being triggered. It so happens that one of the owners of one of the aforementioned restaurants and one of the retail merchants are noted in the investigative report, but no SAR was completed because there was not enough evidence to support a "suspicious" label after the completion of the internal investigation. The case ends there.

In a separate situation in another bank, the fraud unit becomes aware of an elderly female who has been making wire transfers to an individual account held at another bank. Each transfer is in the range of $25,000 to $40,000. When ultimately questioned about her transfers, she claims that she has met a man, who is currently out of the country, who she believes she has established a romantic relationship with and that he will soon be coming to visit her. The elderly female's bank strongly suspects that its customer is the victim of an online "romance scam." After several conversations with her, the elderly female becomes upset that the bank is questioning her newfound boyfriend's validity. Because of an abundance of caution, the bank will not perform any more wire transfers for her. However, the elderly female is provided with a new set of instructions by her newfound boyfriend. Those instructions simply state that the elderly female make withdrawals from her account and send a wire from Western Union to his bank account. The bank finds itself in a position where it believes that its customer is a victim and will lose all her money; however, the bank cannot prevent the customer from taking out her funds. The bank subsequently completes a SAR.

> **Note**
> If that situation should happen at your bank, in addition to completing a SAR, it would be advisable to contact law enforcement by phone ASAP. By the time a SAR goes through the process and gets read by law enforcement, it just might be too late to save the elderly female from losing all her money. In this example, the sooner law enforcement knows, the sooner it can respond. It is OK to contact law enforcement about this situation as long as you still complete a SAR and send it in.

During this time, the AML unit completed a SAR based on the structuring of cash deposits by an individual with the same name as the "boyfriend" of the elderly female. Three times in the two months prior to this SAR being completed, a currency transaction report (CTR) was completed on an individual who lived at the same address as the "boyfriend" who ultimately deposited between $12,000 and $18,000 in cash each time into the same account.

When law enforcement was finally notified and began looking into the situation, it discovered that these incidents were the result of a small organized criminal element that was running various Internet scams targeting the elderly. There were numerous victims involved, and no, there was never any real "boyfriend." Sadly, even after the arrest, most of the funds were not able to be recovered, and several elderly people lost huge chunks of their savings. If the compliance situation had been different and it was set up so that the fraud unit and the AML unit shared information, the chances of this situation being recognized sooner would have been enhanced greatly, perhaps so many elderly people would not have lost so much of their nest eggs. I am glad to see that many financial institutions are now moving in that direction.

Merging the Fraud and AML Units

This brings us to the concept of FRAML—a combination of fraud and anti-money laundering. Historically, financial institutions investigated incidents by sending them to either the fraud unit or the AML unit. There was a large separation of duties, and in turn, the sharing of information across business lines suffered. All information flowed up and down different funnels. On the bank flow chart, the fraud unit was in a different silo than the AML folks. The fraud unit and the AML unit did not share information, they did not use the same software, and they rarely communicated with each other. As a member of law enforcement who attended many high-level bank/regulator/law enforcement meetings and seminars, I personally (as did many of my law enforcement brethren) whined about the ludicrous nature of the situation. What do you think the guys who are committing the credit card frauds have to do with the proceeds of their crime? Of course, they have to launder it. When law enforcement would start looking into the aforementioned situations, they would notice the same names popping up, as well as the same addresses, phone numbers, and other information. No kidding! What a shock! It did not take a brain surgeon to realize that bad guys who commit crimes, including frauds involving a financial institution, must somehow launder the money. Yet, there was a fraud unit in Tampa that never spoke to the AML people in New York. (I just made up those two locations.) The bad guys must have been sipping Dom Perignon and eating Beluga caviar. The bad guys didn't have to worry about building speed bumps and creating barriers to make it more difficult to track them; we were doing it ourselves. How lucky could they get?

Finally, with the assistance of a huge regulator push, many financial institutions started to merge their fraud and AML units. At a minimum, they were allowing their fraud investigators to sit in on some of the AML meetings, and vice versa. This makes all the sense in the world, especially considering that now the new e-filing SARs specifically request information about the possible predicate offense. The SAR form provides a drop-down list of potential illegal activities. Therefore, the more you understand the various unlawful activities, the more thoroughly you can answer the questions on the SAR. Eventually financial institutions began to put both of these units under the umbrella of a new entity called the Financial Crimes Unit, Financial Intelligence Unit, or simply under the Compliance banner. Whatever the official name, the concept is what is important. Now there is a system where information is available and shared with other units. It is possible that the pieces of the puzzle will come together quicker and more clearly now that a financial institution can review all the available intelligence. Integrating and combining cases involving possible fraud or money laundering makes all the sense in the world. Perhaps part of the problem was that we had all sorts of different names for these issues. However, they all have one commonality; they are all crimes. Therefore, perhaps it is easier to comprehend if all the various issues fall under the name Crime. Be it tax evasion, terrorist financing, money laundering, or fraud, they are all crimes. The name Financial Crime Unit makes sense to me. Creating a system where we can put all our financial investigative tools into one big tool box would be a treamendous assest. To Team Good Guy. To make it even more attractive, especially to the budget folks, some of the basic training functions could be combined so as to save resources and also to introduce members of the various teams to facilitate future teamwork. Additionally, if members of both sides of the house (fraud/AML) had a basic understanding of the topics and were cross-trained, in certain situations manpower could be shifted temporarily to accommodate the particular set of circumstances. Further, the use of cross-channel or cross silo alerts could potentially set off alarms in multiple sides of the house and thereby increase the chances of detection.

One thing that financial institutions need to be careful about, if they have or will place both the AML and fraud units under the same umbrella, is the confidentiality of the investigation. It should be noted that the fraud side of the house tends to work with their customers and may have direct contact (usually via phone) with a customer. In an AML investigation, the financial institution is analyzing their customers and their activity. This is always done in strict confidence. In other words, a merged unit needs to be careful about what side of the house they are working on.

One may wonder, why did this convergence not happen in the past? I'm pretty sure that I am hardly the first person to recognize this deficiency and pipe up about it. I cannot provide first-hand evidence; however, in my opinion, it all comes down to cost. What a shock! In a fraud unit, the investigation, detection, and deterrence plans all involve saving money from being taken from the bank. With respect to money laundering, technically there is no loss of funds to the bank. In fact, banks actually make money in a money-laundering operation. Because of such, budgets were created accordingly. Up until the more recent regulatory fines (2012 and on), the risk was well worth the reward for the banks. Before 2012, money being laundered at the bank was a profitable enterprise for the bank. Somewhat surprisingly, few bankers have ever gone to jail for any money-laundering indiscretions. If that's the case, why not take the chance? Subsequent to the actions of 2012, that has changed. Banks are getting hammered by the various regulators with significant fines. In addition to the fines, mandatory remediation costs prove quite costly to the institution. Finally, the risk may not be worth the reward. Well, it's about time!

Law Enforcement's Role

Law enforcement has to exercise patience and understanding at this stage. Depending upon the size and nature of the financial institution, the compliance staff's involvement varies. At a smaller institution, the compliance staff may do it all. They perform opening know your customer operations, monitor transactions, investigate alerts, handle potential fraud or money-laundering issues, write the SARs, and even clean up the place at night. At larger financial institutions, there may be many various silos. Each employee may see only a small piece of the proverbial pie. An employee on the front end (commonly referred to as the *first line of defense*) may never investigate anything. By the same token, the staff that investigates (the second line of defense) may kick up the paperwork surrounding the incident and will never know if yet another silo completed and submitted a SAR. If law enforcement could put themselves in the shoes of the financial institution investigator or analyst for a few moments, law enforcement would make the following observations. First, the employee (let's assume he is working under the compliance banner) sees only a miniscule part of the entire picture.

- He knows nothing of predicate crimes that may be involved with the money on account in his institution in the name of a particular customer.

- He is not aware of any other financial institution's cases.

- He does not know all the information that law enforcement knows.

- When the financial institution submits a SAR, the financial institution may never hear from law enforcement and thereby are not aware if what they did was helpful or not or if the incident was even investigated.

Human nature dictates that people like to be recognized for a job well done. In the current setup, an employee of a financial institution may never know if what he did ever amounted to anything. This can sometimes leave them with the feeling of uselessness. Why bother working so hard if no one ever looks at this stuff?

This is a big issue. In cases from larger financial institutions where there are numerous units under the financial crimes umbrella, not only will an employee not know if law enforcement ever adopted a case, but the employee may never know if their own institution wrote a SAR. This makes it tough to keep an employee's interest. Ironically, the financial institution preaches to its employees about how important the duties of anti-money laundering are; however, it's not important enough for the lower-level employee to know more about the situation once they have completed their job and escalated the matter. You should understand that the financial institution keeps the information provided by their employees confidential all the way up the chain of command. The reason that employees usually never hear anything about the incident again is because of strict confidentiality. It would just not be a good idea to have too many people knowing about a potential law enforcement investigation (assuming the SAR got that far). Now, with that being said, I would like to see some sort of recognition for employees who do an outstanding job. Perhaps specific cases could not be mentioned, but an overall merit award just to have an employee feel that what they do is important would go a long way for their ego.

Picture this: An assembly-line worker at an auto plant puts the steering wheel onto each car frame that comes down the line. That's all he does, and he does it very well. However, he never gets to even see what final product looks like. He is told to keep on doing that job, day after day after day. At some point (and this is strictly my nonmedical doctor opinion), he will become bored and unsatisfied, never knowing if what he does really matters. Does anyone even care? How long do you think he will keep up high standards when his morale is crushed? He needs a pat on the back, a symbol that what he does matters, inspiration to keep up the good work, or something to feel good about. That would be up to bank management to assure that what employees do is very important, and it does get reviewed by law enforcement; indeed, many cases have been made based upon their good work. Whenever I get the chance to speak directly to low-level employees, I make it a point to let them know just how important their role in the AML world is. The AML staff always seems to be quite appreciative to discover that what they do is not for naught. A little acknowledgment and recognition go a long way.

Reasons for crime Crimes are usually committed for one of four reasons:

- *Greed (money, power, and position all fall under this category)*
- *Passion (revenge)*
- *Insanity*
- *Terrorism (cause)*

Of these reasons, approximately 95 percent of all criminal activity is committed for greed. Of the 95 percent resulting from greed, approximately 95 percent of that is committed by some form of organized criminal element.

Note: There is a tendency to think of organized crime as simply the most well-known traditional Italian crime families. Don't be fooled by this. Just about every ethnicity has an organized criminal element. For example, there is a Russian mob, Yakuza, Triads, Irish mob, and Nigerian mob. How about street gangs such as the Bloods, Crypts, and Latin Kings? And I can't leave out outlaw motorcycle gangs and skinheads. Let's not forget the various drug lords. These are all forms of organized crime.

So, in doing the math here, most crimes are committed for the purposes of greed, and most of the people who commit those crimes are involved in some form of organized criminal enterprise.

Now that you have a handle on who commits crimes, then you must connect the dots and realize that most of those crimes must have their illegally obtained funds laundered. This is why money laundering is close to a $2 trillion a year business.

A Suggestion for Dealing with Your Own Personnel

Since it appears difficult or unlikely that any financial institution violators will ever be prosecuted and sent to jail, there is something else that really irks me. When some of these employees are fired, forced to resign, or resign on their own because of an AML indiscretion, some of these people have ended up working at another financial institution. How crazy is that (forgiving those who resigned on their own because they did not agree with the bank policies)? My suggestion is to create policy much like in the broker/dealer world. Every broker/dealer must be licensed through the Security Exchange Commission (SEC). If a broker wants to work in the investment world, the broker needs a license. If they screw up (within certain parameters) along the way, their license can be revoked. That would prevent the violators from ever working at the broker/dealer across the street or any other broker/dealer for that matter. Why not make certain-level bankers obtain a banking license? Then if things go south as a result of their own indiscretions, their licenses can be revoked, and you never have to be concerned that the violator will be rearing his ugly head at the bank across the street or anywhere else.

Types of Fraud

Some of the more common types of fraudulent crimes that might be seen by the financial institution and documented as such are as follows:

- Bribery

- Credit card/debit card/stored value card
- Embezzlement
- Extortion
- Forgery
- Healthcare fraud
- Identity theft
- Insurance fraud
- Mail fraud
- Mortgage fraud
- Ponzi schemes
- Securities fraud
- Tax evasion
- Telemarketing fraud
- Wire fraud

These crimes are all some form of larceny.[1] Fraud usually involves a form of larceny in that frauds usually involve some form of deception or a violation of a position of trust.

Summary

By now you should understand that to have the crime of money laundering, there has to be a predicate crime. Crimes such as gambling, prostitution, and drug dealing may not be easy to decipher. However, the general rules of money-laundering red flags should provide guidance. A financial institution may never know exactly what the predicate crime is; that is something for law enforcement to determine. When we shift to the possibility of the predicate crime being some type of fraud, then there is a good chance that the financial institution will observe some commonalities and address the incident as a fraud event. Regardless of the predicate crime, most all crimes involving money or value will at some point cross the money-laundering bridge.

Footnotes

1 *Larceny*: New York State penal code section 155.05 states the following: Larceny includes a wrongful

taking, obtaining, or withholding of another's property.

Money-Laundering Red Flags

Potentially Suspicious Activity That May Indicate Money Laundering

✉

(1)

This content of this appendix on various red flags comes from the Federal Financial Institution Examination Council (

www.ffiec.gov/bsa_aml_infobase/documents/BSA_AML_Man_2014.pdf , pages F-1 to F-9).

Customers Who Provide Insufficient or Suspicious Information

- A customer uses unusual or suspicious identification documents that cannot be readily verified.

- A customer provides an individual taxpayer identification number after having previously used a Social Security number.

- A customer uses different taxpayer identification numbers with variations of his or her name.

- A business is reluctant, when establishing a new account, to provide complete information about the nature and purpose of its business, anticipated account activity, prior banking relationships, the names of its officers and directors, or information on its business location.

- A customer's home or business telephone is disconnected.

- The customer's background differs from that which would be expected on the basis of his or her business activities.

- A customer makes frequent or large transactions and has no record of past or present employment experience.

- A customer is a trust, shell company, or Private Investment Company that is reluctant to provide information on controlling parties and underlying beneficiaries. Beneficial owners may hire nominee incorporation services to establish shell companies and open bank accounts for those shell companies while shielding the owner's identity.

Efforts to Avoid Reporting or Recordkeeping Requirement

- A customer or group tries to persuade a bank employee not to file required reports or maintain required records.

- A customer is reluctant to provide information needed to file a mandatory report, to have the report filed, or to proceed with a transaction after being informed that the report must be filed.

- A customer is reluctant to furnish identification when purchasing negotiable instruments in recordable amounts.

- A business or customer asks to be exempted from reporting or record keeping requirements.

- A person customarily uses the automated teller machine to make several bank deposits below a specified threshold.

- A customer deposits funds into several accounts, usually in amounts of less than $3,000, which are subsequently consolidated into a master account and transferred outside of the country, particularly to or through a location of specific concern (e.g., countries designated by national authorities and Financial Action Task Force on Money Laundering (FATF) as non-cooperative countries and territories).

- A customer accesses a safe deposit box after completing a transaction involving a large withdrawal of currency, or accesses a safe deposit box before making currency deposits structured at or just under $10,000, to evade CTR filing requirements.

Funds Transfers

- Many funds transfers are sent in large, round dollar, hundred dollar, or thousand dollar amounts.

- Funds transfer activity occurs to or from a financial secrecy haven, or to or from a higher-risk geographic location without an apparent business reason or when the activity is inconsistent with the customer's business or history.

- Funds transfer activity occurs to or from a financial institution located in a higher risk jurisdiction distant from the customer's operations.

- Many small, incoming transfers of funds are received, or deposits are made using checks and money orders. Almost immediately, all or most of the transfers or deposits are wired to another city or country in a manner inconsistent with the customer's business or history.

- Large, incoming funds transfers are received on behalf of a foreign client, with little or no explicit reason.

- Funds transfer activity is unexplained, repetitive, or shows unusual patterns.

- Payments or receipts with no apparent links to legitimate contracts, goods, or services are received.

- Funds transfers are sent or received from the same person to or from different accounts.

- Funds transfers contain limited content and lack related party information.

Automated Clearing House Transactions

- Large-value, automated clearing house (ACH) transactions are frequently initiated through third-party service providers (TPSP) by originators that are not bank customers and for which the bank has no or insufficient due diligence.

- TPSPs have a history of violating ACH network rules or generating illegal transactions, or processing manipulated or fraudulent transactions on behalf of their customers.

- Multiple layers of TPSPs that appear to be unnecessarily involved in transactions.

- Unusually high level of transactions initiated over the Internet or by telephone.

- NACHA — The Electronic Payments Association (NACHA) information requests indicate potential concerns with the bank's usage of the ACH system.

Activity Inconsistent with the Customer's Business

- The currency transaction patterns of a business show a sudden change inconsistent with normal activities.

- A large volume of cashier's checks, money orders, or funds transfers is deposited into, or purchased through, an account when the nature of the accountholder's business would not appear to justify such activity.

- A retail business has dramatically different patterns of currency deposits from similar businesses in the same general location.

- Unusual transfers of funds occur among related accounts or among accounts that involve the same or related principals.

- The owner of both a retail business and a check-cashing service does not ask for currency when depositing checks, possibly indicating the availability of another source of currency.

- Goods or services purchased by the business do not match the customer's stated line of business.

- Payments for goods or services are made by checks, money orders, or bank drafts not drawn from the account of the entity that made the purchase.

Lending Activity

- Loans secured by pledged assets held by third parties unrelated to the borrower.

- Loan secured by deposits or other readily marketable assets, such as securities, particularly when owned by apparently unrelated third parties.

- Borrower defaults on a cash-secured loan or any loan that is secured by assets that are readily convertible into currency.

- Loans are made for, or are paid on behalf of, a third party with no reasonable explanation.

- To secure a loan, the customer purchases a certificate of deposit using an unknown source of funds, particularly when funds are provided via currency or multiple monetary instruments.

- Loans that lack a legitimate business purpose, provide the bank with significant fees for assuming little or no risk, or tend to obscure the movement of funds (e.g., loans made to a borrower and immediately sold to an entity related to the borrower).

Changes in Bank-to-Bank Transactions

- The size and frequency of currency deposits increases rapidly with no corresponding increase in non-currency deposits.

- A bank is unable to track the true accountholder of correspondent or concentration account transactions.

- The turnover in large-denomination bills is significant and appears uncharacteristic, given the bank's location.

- Changes in currency-shipment patterns between correspondent banks are significant.

Cross-Border Financial Institution Transactions

- U.S. bank increases sales or exchanges of large denomination U.S. bank notes to Mexican financial institution(s).

- Large volumes of small denomination U.S. banknotes being sent from Mexican casas de cambio to their U.S. accounts via armored transport or sold directly to U.S. banks. These sales or exchanges may involve jurisdictions outside of Mexico.

- Casas de cambio direct the remittance of funds via multiple funds transfers to jurisdictions outside of Mexico that bear no apparent business relationship with the casas de cambio. Funds transfer recipients may include individuals, businesses, and other entities in free trade zones.

- Casas de cambio deposit numerous third-party items, including sequentially numbered monetary instruments, to their accounts at U.S. banks.

- Casas de cambio direct the remittance of funds transfers from their accounts at Mexican financial institutions to accounts at U.S. banks. These funds transfers follow the deposit of currency and third-party items by the casas de cambio into their Mexican financial institution.

Bulk Currency Shipments

- An increase in the sale of large denomination U.S. bank notes to foreign financial institutions by U.S. banks.

- Large volumes of small denomination U.S. bank notes being sent from foreign nonbank financial institutions to their accounts in the United States via armored transport, or sold directly to U.S. banks.

- Multiple wire transfers initiated by foreign nonbank financial institutions that direct U.S. banks to remit funds to other jurisdictions that bear no apparent business relationship with that foreign nonbank financial institution. Recipients may include individuals, businesses, and other entities in free trade zones and other locations.

- The exchange of small denomination U.S. bank notes for large denomination U.S. bank notes that may be sent to foreign countries.

- Deposits by foreign nonbank financial institutions to their accounts at U.S. banks that include third-party items, including sequentially numbered monetary instruments.

- Deposits of currency and third-party items by foreign nonbank financial institutions to their accounts at foreign financial institutions and thereafter direct wire transfers to the foreign nonbank financial institution's accounts at U.S. banks.

Trade Finance

- Items shipped that are inconsistent with the nature of the customer's business (e.g., a steel company that starts dealing in paper products, or an information technology company that starts dealing in bulk pharmaceuticals).

- Customers conducting business in higher-risk jurisdictions.

- Customers shipping items through higher-risk jurisdictions, including transit through non-cooperative countries.

- Customers involved in potentially higher-risk activities, including activities that may be subject to export/import restrictions (e.g., equipment for military or police organizations of foreign governments, weapons, ammunition, chemical mixtures, classified defense articles, sensitive technical data, nuclear materials, precious gems, or certain natural resources such as metals, ore, and crude oil).

- Obvious over, or, under-pricing of goods and services.

- Obvious misrepresentation of quantity or type of goods imported or exported.

- Transaction structure appears unnecessarily complex and designed to obscure the true nature of the transaction.

- Customer requests payment of proceeds to an unrelated third party.

- Shipment locations or description of goods not consistent with letter of credit.

- Significantly amended letters of credit without reasonable justification or changes to the beneficiary or location of payment. Any changes in the names of parties should prompt additional OFAC review.

Privately Owned Automated Teller Machines

- Automated teller machine (ATM) activity levels are high in comparison with other privately owned or bank-owned ATMs in comparable geographic and demographic locations.

- Sources of currency for the ATM cannot be identified or confirmed through withdrawals from account, armored car contracts, lending arrangements, or other appropriate documentation.

Insurance

- A customer purchases products with termination features without concern for the product's investment performance.

- A customer purchases insurance products using a single, large premium payment, particularly when payment is made through unusual methods such as currency or currency equivalents.

- A customer purchases a product that appears outside the customer's normal range of financial wealth or estate planning needs.

- A customer borrows against the cash surrender value of permanent life insurance policies, particularly when payments are made to apparently unrelated third parties.

- Policies are purchased that allow for the transfer of beneficial ownership interests without the knowledge and consent of the insurance issuer. This would include secondhand endowment and bearer insurance policies.

- A customer is known to purchase several insurance products and uses the proceeds from an early policy surrender to purchase other financial assets.

- A customer uses multiple currency equivalents (e.g., cashier's checks and money orders) from different banks and money services businesses to make insurance policy or annuity payments.

Shell Company Activity

- A bank is unable to obtain sufficient information or information is unavailable to positively identify originators or beneficiaries of accounts or other banking activity (using Internet, commercial database searches, or direct inquiries to a respondent bank).

- Payments to or from the company have no stated purpose, do not reference goods or services, or identify only a contract or invoice number.

- Goods or services, if identified, do not match profile of company provided by respondent bank or character of the financial activity; a company references remarkably dissimilar goods and services in related funds transfers; explanation given by foreign respondent bank is inconsistent with observed funds transfer activity.

- Transacting businesses share the same address, provide only a registered agent's address, or have other address inconsistencies.

- Unusually large number and variety of beneficiaries are receiving funds transfers from one company.

- Frequent involvement of multiple jurisdictions or beneficiaries located in higher-risk offshore financial centers.

- A foreign correspondent bank exceeds the expected volume in its client profile for funds transfers, or an individual company exhibits a high volume and pattern of funds transfers that is inconsistent with its normal business activity.

- Multiple high-value payments or transfers between shell companies with no apparent legitimate business purpose.

- Purpose of the shell company is unknown or unclear.

Embassy and Foreign Consulate Accounts

- Official embassy business is conducted through personal accounts.

- Account activity is not consistent with the purpose of the account, such as pouch activity or payable upon proper identification transactions.

- Accounts are funded through substantial currency transactions.

- Accounts directly fund personal expenses of foreign nationals without appropriate controls, including, but not limited to, expenses for college students.

- **Employees**

- Employee exhibits a lavish lifestyle that cannot be supported by his or her salary.

- Employee fails to conform to recognized policies, procedures, and processes, particularly in private banking.

- Employee is reluctant to take a vacation.

- Employee overrides a hold placed on an account identified as suspicious so that transactions can occur in the account.

Other Unusual or Suspicious Customer Activity

- Customer frequently exchanges small-dollar denominations for large-dollar denominations.

- Customer frequently deposits currency wrapped in currency straps or currency wrapped in rubber bands that is disorganized and does not balance when counted.

- Customer purchases a number of cashier's checks, money orders, or traveler's checks for large amounts under a specified threshold.

- Customer purchases a number of open-end prepaid cards for large amounts. Purchases of prepaid cards are not commensurate with normal business activities.

- Customer receives large and frequent deposits from online payments systems yet has no apparent online or auction business.

- Monetary instruments deposited by mail are numbered sequentially or have unusual symbols or stamps on them.

- Suspicious movements of funds occur from one bank to another, and then funds are moved back to the first bank.

- Deposits are structured through multiple branches of the same bank or by groups of people who enter a single branch at the same time.

- Currency is deposited or withdrawn in amounts just below identification or reporting thresholds.

- Customer visits a safe deposit box or uses a safe custody account on an unusually frequent basis.

- Safe deposit boxes or safe custody accounts opened by individuals who do not reside or work in the institution's service area, despite the availability of such services at an institution closer to them.

- Customer repeatedly uses a bank or branch location that is geographically distant from the customer's home or office without sufficient business purpose.

- Customer exhibits unusual traffic patterns in the safe deposit box area or unusual use of safe custody accounts. For example, several individuals arrive together, enter frequently, or carry bags or other containers that could conceal large amounts of currency, monetary instruments, or small valuable items.

- Customer rents multiple safe deposit boxes to store large amounts of currency, monetary instruments, or high-value assets awaiting conversion to currency, for placement into the banking system. Similarly, a customer establishes multiple safe custody accounts to park large amounts of securities awaiting sale and conversion into currency, monetary instruments, outgoing funds transfers, or a combination thereof, for placement into the banking system.

- Unusual use of trust funds in business transactions or other financial activity.

- Customer uses a personal account for business purposes.

- Customer has established multiple accounts in various corporate or individual names that lack sufficient business purpose for the account complexities or appear to be an effort to hide the beneficial ownership from the bank.

- Customer makes multiple and frequent currency deposits to various accounts that are purportedly unrelated.

- Customer conducts large deposits and withdrawals during a short time period after opening and then subsequently closes the account or the account becomes dormant. Conversely, an account with little activity may suddenly experience large deposit and withdrawal activity.

- Customer makes high-value transactions not commensurate with the customer's known incomes.

Code of Federal Regulations Title 31 Section 103.18

---

§ 103.18 Reports by banks of suspicious transactions.

(a) General. (1) Every bank shall file with the Treasury Department, to the extent and in the manner required by this section, a report of any suspicious transaction relevant to a possible violation of law or regulation. A bank may also file with the Treasury Department by using the Suspicious Activity Report specified in paragraph (b)(1) of this section or otherwise, a report of any suspicious transaction that it believes is relevant to the possible violation of any law or regulation but whose reporting is not required by this section.

(2) A transaction requires reporting under the terms of this section if it is conducted or attempted by, at, or through the bank, it involves or aggregates at least $5,000 in funds or other assets, and the bank knows, suspects, or has reason to suspect that: (i) The transaction involves funds derived from illegal activities or is intended or conducted in order to hide or disguise funds or assets derived from illegal activities (including, without limitation, the ownership, nature, source, location, or control of such funds or assets) as part of a plan to violate or evade any federal law or regulation or to avoid any transaction reporting requirement under federal law or regulation; (ii) The transaction is designed to evade any requirements of this part or of any other regulations promulgated under the Bank Secrecy Act, Pub. L. 91-508, as amended, codified at 12 U.S.C. 1829b, 12 U.S.C. 1951--1959, and 31 U.S.C. 5311--5330; or (iii) The transaction has no business or apparent lawful purpose or is not the sort in which the particular customer would normally be expected to engage, and the bank knows of no reasonable explanation for the transaction after examining the available facts, including the background and possible purpose of the transaction.

(b) Filing procedures--(1) What to file. A suspicious transaction shall be reported by completing a Suspicious Activity Report ("SAR") and collecting and maintaining supporting documentation as required by paragraph (d) of this section.

(2) Where to file. The SAR shall be filed with FinCEN in a central location, to be determined by FinCEN, as indicated in the instructions to the SAR.

(3) When to file. A bank is required to file a SAR no later than 30 calendar days after the date of initial detection by the bank of facts that may constitute a basis for filing a SAR. If no suspect was identified on the date of the detection of the incident requiring the filing, a bank may delay filing a SAR for an additional 30 calendar days to identify a suspect. In no case shall reporting be delayed more than 60 calendar days after the date of initial detection of a reportable transaction. In situations involving violations that require immediate attention, such as, for example, ongoing money laundering schemes, the bank shall immediately notify, by telephone, an appropriate law enforcement authority in addition to filing timely a SAR.

(c) Exceptions. A bank is not required to file a SAR for a robbery or burglary committed or attempted that is reported to appropriate law enforcement authorities, or for lost, missing, counterfeit, or stolen securities with respect to which the bank files a report pursuant to the reporting requirements of 17 CFR 240.17f-1.

(d) Retention of records. A bank shall maintain a copy of any SAR filed and the original or business record equivalent of any supporting documentation for a period of five years from the date of filing the SAR. Supporting documentation shall be identified, and maintained by the bank as such, and shall be deemed to have been filed with the SAR. A bank shall make all supporting documentation available to FinCEN and any appropriate law enforcement agencies or bank supervisory agencies upon request.

(e) Confidentiality of reports; limitation of liability. No bank or other financial institution, and no director, officer, employee, or agent of any bank or other financial institution, who reports a suspicious transaction under this part, may notify any person involved in the transaction that the transaction has been reported. Thus, any person subpoenaed or otherwise requested to disclose a SAR or the information contained in a SAR, except where such disclosure is requested by FinCEN or an appropriate law enforcement or bank supervisory agency, shall decline to produce the SAR or to provide any information that would disclose that a SAR has been prepared or filed, citing this paragraph (e) and 31 U.S.C. 5318(g)(2), and shall notify FinCEN of any such request and its response thereto. A bank, and any director, officer, employee, or agent of such bank, that makes a report pursuant to this section (whether such report is required by this section or is made voluntarily) shall be protected from liability for any disclosure contained in, or for failure to disclose the fact of such report, or both, to the full extent provided by 31 U.S.C. 5318(g)(3).

(f) Compliance. Compliance with this section shall be audited by the Department of the Treasury, through FinCEN or its delegees under the terms of the Bank Secrecy Act. Failure to satisfy the requirements of this section may be a violation of the reporting rules of the Bank Secrecy Act and of this part. Such failure may also violate provisions of Title 12 of the Code of Federal Regulations.

[Codified to 31 C.F.R. § 103.18]

Glossary

account A business relationship between a financial institution and its customer.

alternative remittance systems Also called parallel or underground banking systems. They are unregulated, uninsured, and unmonitored systems that often do not maintain any documentation. Usually they involve fund transfers. These are typically ethnic based and go by different names according to the country/culture. In Pakistan it is referred to as a hawala; in India, a hundi; and in China, fei ch'ien.

AML Anti-money laundering.

appropriate authorities Sometimes referred to as competent authorities. This is a term for regulators, accrediting institutions, certain law enforcement agencies, and officials and prosecutorial agencies.

audit Reviewing policies and procedures, transactions, and account information and attempting to determine the accuracy of compliance according to the standards provided.

Basel committee Created by the governors of the central banks in 1974 in Basel, Switzerland. These committees develop supervisory standards and provide guidance to the central banks.

batch transfer When several wire transfers are sent to the same financial institution from one financial institution. These batch transfers may or may not be designated for the same person/entity.

bearer shares Negotiable instruments granting ownership to the person who possesses the particular bearer share certificate.

beneficial owner Also called ultimate beneficial owner. This is a person (not a corporation) who ultimately controls an account or the person on whose behalf a transaction is being conducted.

beneficiary financial institution The financial institution that receives a wire transfer.

BSA Bank Secrecy Act. This is the basis of AML programs. First created in 1970, it requires banks to maintain records in the form of completed currency transaction reports and suspicious activity reports.

casa de cambio Spanish for currency exchange. This is a money services business.

CDD Customer due diligence. This is the process of identifying the customer on the basis of documents, data, or information obtained from a reliable and independent source and understanding the purpose of the account.

CFT Countering the financing of terror.

CIP Customer identification program. All financial institutions must gather and maintain records of their customers' names, dates of birth, addresses, and identification numbers (such as Social Security numbers [SSNs]).

concentration accounts Also called clearing or omnibus accounts. These are used by a bank for bank-to-bank or administrative transactions.

concentration risk The risk of having too much money exposed to certain categories of customers and the possibility of something happening to their positions.

correspondent banking Banking services by one bank to another bank (correspondent to respondent). This type of banking was created to receive deposits from or make payments on behalf of a foreign financial institution that has no physical presence in the United States.

CTF Counter-terror financing.

CTR Currency transaction report. Any cash transaction over $10,000 must have a currency transaction report completed and forwarded to FinCEN.

designated nonfinancial businesses and professions Can include casinos; dealers in precious metals or stones; real estate agents; lawyers, notaries, and other independent legal professionals and accountants; and trust and company service providers.

EDD Enhanced due diligence. This is the process of investigating with greater scrutiny or "drilling down" further to ascertain additional information about a subject or entity. This is the next level after CDD.

Egmont Group International association of various countries' financial intelligence units (FIUs). The group promotes cooperation among FIUs.

FATF Financial Action Task Force. This is an organization consisting of member countries that develop measures for international money-laundering best practices, referred to as the FATF 40 recommendations (plus 9 special recommendations of terrorist financing). Additionally, FATF conducts mutual peer reviews of its member countries and publishes numerous reports and white papers on a variety of associated topics.

financial institution Includes any person or entity doing business in one or more of the following capacities: bank, broker or dealer in securities, money services business, telegraph company, casino, card club, or person subject to supervision by any state or federal bank supervisory authority.

FinCEN Financial Crimes Enforcement Network. This is a bureau of the U.S. Treasury created in 1990 as the U.S. financial intelligence unit. It coordinates information gathering (all financial institution reporting forms such as SARs and CTRs are sent here) that is analyzed and made available to appropriate regulating bodies and law enforcement.

FIU Financial intelligence unit. For a country, this is a central department responsible for receiving and analyzing information from financial institutions and disseminating it to competent authorities, such as regulators and law enforcement.

free trade zones Designated areas within countries that provide a free trade area with little regulation.

gatekeepers Professionals who may have control over an individual's or entity's funds. Lawyers, accountants, and investment advisors are all considered gatekeepers.

HIFCA High-intensity financial crimes area. There are seven HIFCAs in the United States designated as a regional area of money-laundering concern.

high-risk indicator A trigger or alert that notifies of a possible unusual event or red flag that could potentially lead to a SAR. Typically the event must be investigated and then cleared or escalated.

high-risk review An analysis and review of an account rated as high risk.

inherent risk The risk to an entity despite actions that management might take to alter the risk's likelihood or impact. Inherent risk usually results from the business choices of an institution.

integration The third stage of money laundering. After the illegally obtained funds are moved around and distanced from their origin, they are then made available to the money launderer as "clean" funds.

KYC Know your customer. KYC consists of policies and procedures that require financial institutions to conduct due diligence on all new customers to determine and verify their identity, source of funds, and nature of their business.

layering The second stage of money laundering. After illegally obtained funds are "placed" into the financial system, they are moved, dispersed, and disguised frequently as to cloud the money trail and create distance from the origin.

legal entities Companies, trusts, banks, and partnerships. Offshore private companies present a higher risk.

legal risk If financial institutions are used as vehicles for illegal activities by customers, the institutions face the risk of fines and penalties.

microstructuring A form of structuring that reduces the transactions to much smaller amounts. Amounts from $500 to $2,000 are typical microstructuring ranges.

monetary instruments Bank checks or drafts, cashier's check, money orders, and traveler's checks.

NCCT Noncooperative countries or territories. These are countries designated by FATF as repeatedly disregarding the issues of money laundering or are unwilling to create or enforce money-laundering regulations in their country. This is sometimes referred to as the black list or the name and shame list.

nonbank financial institution Institutions other than banks that offer financial services such as the following: casinos and card clubs, securities and commodities firms, money services businesses, insurance companies, loan or finance companies, operators of credit card systems, and other financial institutions such as dealers in precious metals, stones or jewels, and pawnbrokers.

NPO Nonprofit organization.

OFAC Office of Financial Assets Control. This is a division of the U.S. Department of the Treasury. OFAC administers and enforces economic and trade sanctions based on U.S. foreign policy and national security goals against targeted foreign countries, terrorists, narcotic traffickers, and those engaged in the proliferation of weapons of mass destruction.

operational risk The risk of direct or indirect loss from flawed or failed internal processes, management, or systems.

payable-through account Commonly referred to as a pass-through account. This is an account that allows a respondent bank's customer to access it directly, such as by check writing or making deposits.

PEP Politically exposed person. This is an individual who has or has had a prominent public function, such as a senior politician or military or judicial official, as well as any close family members and close associates.

placement The first stage of money laundering. This is the first time that illegally obtained funds enter the legitimate financial system.

pouch activity Using a courier to transport currency, monetary instruments, or other documents to a financial institution.

residual risk The amount of risk that remains after all controls have been applied to reduce the possibility or impact of the risk.

risk management A quantitative method used for developing and implementing a framework that identifies risk more precisely.

risk matrix A chart used to analyze customer risk based on predetermined variables such as geography and business type.

safe harbor The protection from liability to any financial institution or employee of a financial institution that submits a suspicious activity report.

SAR Suspicious activity report. This is a report generated and completed by a financial institution and subsequently submitted to FinCEN. The report indicates an action that has transpired or an attempt at an action or a behavior that does not make sense or is not commiserate with the usual activity of that customer or of similar customers and professions.

SDN Specially designated national. This is a list of individuals and companies known by the OFAC to be possible money launderers or terrorists.

shell bank A bank incorporated in a jurisdiction in which it has no physical presence and that is not affiliated with a regulated group. The address may come back to a post-office box or a suite. It is a violation to conduct any business with a shell bank.

source of funds The origin of the customer's funds and how such funds are then connected to a customer's source of wealth.

source of wealth How the customer's net worth is or was accumulated.

structuring Organizing financial transactions in such a way as to avoid the creation of certain bank reporting documents. For example, instead of depositing $10,000 (knowing that would create a CTR), the customer instead deposits $9,999. Doing this multiple times in a short time frame may show a specific pattern of deliberate avoidance and constitute structuring.

SUA Specified unlawful activities. These are certain crimes (typically serious felonies) that are committed prior to the charge of money laundering. Sometimes these are referred to as predicate crimes.

terrorism The unlawful use of force or violence against people or property to intimidate or coerce a government, the civilian population, or any segment thereof, in furtherance of political or social objectives.

terrorist organization A group of terrorists that commits, or attempts to commit, terrorist acts by any means directly or indirectly, unlawfully, and willfully.

trade-based money laundering The process of disguising the proceeds of ill-gotten gains and distributing the value through the use of various trade transactions. Typical schemes are under-and over-invoicing, the Black Market Peso Exchange, and underground banking.

trusts A legal entity or arrangement in which assets (usually financial assets or securities) are held by one person (trustee) in trust for the benefit of another person or group of persons (beneficiaries).

Index

A

ACAMS.
  See The Association of Certified Money Laundering Specialists (ACAMS)
Accountants
  in drug case as forensic accounting investigation in money laundering unit
  professional money launderer training, law enforcement
ACFE.
  See The Association of Certified Fraud Examiners (ACFE)
AML.
  See Anti-money laundering (AML)
Annunzio–Wylie Act 1992
  civil liability and harbor provision suspicious activity report
Anti-money laundering (AML) program "alerts"
  customer risk

DCO

drug dealing/arms trading due diligence financial crimes financial institutions

FRAML

fraud team
geographic risk independent audit function internal policies and procedures
law enforcement organizations   *See* (Organizations, AML) Palermo
convention product and service risk program deficiency

CIP

filing procedures high-risk customers identification inadequate policy and
procedures suspicious transaction monitoring training
regulators

CTR

currency transaction exemptions
   reporting
financial institution form 40
law enforcement money laundering
Basel Committee on Banking Supervision

BIS

concerns
description
KYC policy
BIS.
   See Bank for International Settlements (BIS)
Black Market Peso Exchange (BMPE)

BSA

Colombian drug dealer
BMPE.
   See Black Market Peso Exchange (BMPE)
BSA.
   See Bank Secrecy Act (BSA)

C

CFTC.
   See Commodities Futures Trading Commission (CFTC)
Chemists
CHIPS.
   See Clearing House Interbank Payment System (CHIPS)
CIP.
   See Customer identification program (CIP)
Clearing House Interbank Payment System (CHIPS)
CMIRs.
   See Currency or monetary instruments report (CMIRs)

Commodities Futures Trading Commission (CFTC)
Credit card theft ring
CTR.
　　See Currency transaction report (CTR)
Currency or monetary instruments report (CMIRs)
Currency transaction report (CTR)
Customer due diligence (CDD) business risk COMPSTAT process

EDD

financial profile geography risk individual risk investigative checklist law enforcement online customers identification primary and secondary documents product risk reviewers/regulator risk matrix
shell company "voo-due diligence"
Customer identification program (CIP) account-opening documents bank management

CDD

EDD

financial institution/customer relationship intelligence, sources commercial databases FinCEN 314b
in-house systems invisible web portal open source information public records social networks vendor databases investigation mind-set information/technology instincts, investigation JADE rule
smell test implementation

PEPS

transaction-monitoring
Cyber banking
internet
smart cards

D

MLCA

MLSA

Money Laundering and Financial Crimes Act

OFAC

USA PATRIOT Act
Federal Reserve Bank
The Financial Action Task Force (FATF) associate members description
    EU directive FATF 40 recommendations FATF 40 + 9 recommendations goals
    High Risk and Non-Cooperative Jurisdictions list
Financial Crimes Enforcement Network (FinCEN)

CMIR

CTRs
FBARs
SARs
Financial crimes unit (FCU)
Financial Industry Regulatory Authority (FINRA)
Financial institution bank statements canceled checks credit cards/debit cards customer contact reports customer information deposit slips investigative mind, development hypothesis
    instincts
    JADE rule
    smell test, employment suspiciousness money order records regulators
    See (Regulators, financial institution) safe deposit visitation records SAR supporting documents signature cards wire transfers
Financial intelligence unit (FIU)
FinCEN.
    See Financial Crimes Enforcement Network (FinCEN)
FINRA.
    See Financial Industry Regulatory Authority (FINRA)
FIU.
    See Financial intelligence unit (FIU)

Foreign bank and financial accounts (FBARs)
Forensic accounting
FRAML.
See Fraud and AML (FRAML)
Fraud and AML (FRAML) e-filing SARs

FCU

FIU

information, sharing law enforcement money laundering
Fraudulent crimes, financial institution

I, J

IBAN.
See International Bank Account Number (IBAN)
ICE.
See Immigration and Customs Enforcement (ICE)
IMF.
See International Monetary Fund (IMF)
Immigration and Customs Enforcement (ICE)
Independent service operator (ISO)
International Bank Account Number (IBAN)
International Monetary Fund (IMF)
ISO.
See Independent service operator (ISO)

K

Know your customer (KYC) program   *See also* Customer Identification
program (CIP)
KYC.
See Know your customer (KYC) program

L

Law enforcement accountants
    assembly-line worker asset seizure and financial institution.
    See (Financial institution) bankers
    compliance staff first line of defense observations reasons for crime
    regulators.
    See (Regulators, financial institution) SAR power

M

MLCA.
    See Money Laundering Control Act (MLCA)
MLSA.
    See Money Laundering Suppression Act (MLSA)
Money laundering AML efforts

BMPE

    cash smuggling

CMIR

        hidden cash
        ill-gotten cash casinos
        FinCEN
        Nevada Gaming Commission Ticket In and Ticket Out

CIP

        credit card skimmer criminal enterprise organization cyber banking fraud units
        fundamental role drug trafficker insider dealer organized criminal terrorist
        gangster's funds slot machines and laundromats small-denomination bills or
        coins gold
        good/service invoice money orders money service business Palermo
        convention Ponzi (pyramid) schemes reasons, launder regulations
        scams
        stages
            integration

layering
placement
structuring
tax evader/terrorist financier terrorism
transactions trade-based
underground banking system (Hawala)

USPS

wire transfers

BIC

CHIPS

Fedwire

IBAN

offshore bank/Swiss account shell/nominee company SWIFT code
transmitting and receiving financial institutions
Money Laundering and Financial Crimes Strategy Act
Money Laundering Control Act (MLCA)
Money Laundering Suppression Act (MLSA)

N

National Credit Union Administration

O

OCC.
    See The Office of the Comptroller of the Currency (OCC)
OFAC.
    See Office of Foreign Assets and Control (OFAC)
Office of Foreign Assets and Control (OFAC)

The Office of the Comptroller of the Currency (OCC)
Organizations, AML
    Basel Committee on Banking Supervision economic sanctions Egmont
    EU Directive

FATF

IMF

    Transparency International

USA PATRIOT ACT

    Wolfsberg

P, Q
Pathologists
PEPS.
    See Politically exposed persons (PEPS)
Politically exposed persons (PEPS)

FATF

    foreign corruption OFAC sanctions

R

Regulators, financial institution broker/dealer guidance, on rules and regulations
guidelines
    national bank SAR review meetings standards
    state bank
    symbiotic relationship

S

SAR.

USA PATRIOT ACT

anti-terrorism and AML legislation

BSA

extraterritorial impact legislation
section 311
section 312, 313
section 319
U.S. Treasury
USPS.
See U.S. Postal Service (USPS)

W, X, Y, Z

Wolfsberg
and Basel Committee intelligence purposes money-laundering, published
papers "Questionnaire for Correspondent Banking"
stored value cards